# ARMENIA AND KARABAGH

## THE
## STRUGGLE
## FOR
## UNITY

Minority Rights Publications

**Minority Rights Group** is an international, non-governmental organization whose aims are to secure justice for minority (and non-dominant majority) groups suffering discrimination by:

1. Researching and publishing the facts as widely as possible to raise public knowledge and awareness of minority issues worldwide.

2. Advocating on all aspects of the human rights of minorities to aid the prevention of dangerous and destructive conflicts.

3. Educating through its schools programme on issues relating to prejudice, discrimination and group conflicts.

If you would like to know more about the work of the Minority Rights Group, please contact Alan Phillips (Director), MRG, 379 Brixton Road, London SW9 7DE, United Kingdom.

*m*

**Minority Rights Publications** is a new series of books from the Minority Rights Group. Through the series, we aim to make available to a wide audience reliable data on, and objective analyses of, specific minority issues. The series draws on the expertise and authority built up by the Minority Rights Group over two decades of publishing. Further details on MRG's highly acclaimed series of reports can be found at the end of this book. Other titles in the book series are:

The Balkans: Minorities and States in Conflict
by Hugh Poulton (1991)

*forthcoming titles will cover:*
Refugees in Europe
The Kurds

# ARMENIA AND KARABAGH

## THE STRUGGLE FOR UNITY

Edited by
Christopher J. Walker

Foreword by
Gérard Chaliand

Minority Rights Publications

© Minority Rights Group 1991

First published in Great Britain
in 1991 by
Minority Rights Publications
379 Brixton Road
London SW9 7DE

British Library Cataloguing in Publication Data
A CIP catalogue record of this book is available from the British Library

ISBN 1 873194 00 5 paper
ISBN 1 873194 20 X hardback

Library of Congress Cataloguing in Publication Data
CIP Data available from the Library of Congress

Designed and typeset by Brixton Graphics
Printed and bound by Billing and Sons Ltd

Cover photo of Armenians in Leninakan –
D. Brinicombe / The Hutchison Library

# CONTENTS

# FOREWORD

### by Gérard Chaliand

The deportation and massacre of whole communities of Armenians in the Ottoman Empire in 1915 was not only an Armenian tragedy, but also briefly shocked the international conscience. For a long time it was forgotten by the outside world. Today it is regarded as the first genocide of the 20th Century.

At the time of the war and in the wake of serious military reversals, the pan-Turkist (or pan-Turanian) government of the Young Turks determined a drastic solution to the 'Armenian question'. Having already lost the Balkans and Libya in previous conflicts, the Young Turk government feared losing the empire's north-eastern provinces, where the majority of the Armenian population lived, to a Russian advance. Therefore it was decided to liquidate the Armenian population. In the course of the massacres and deportations which followed, about one and a half million Armenians perished, and about half a million Armenians became refugees.

Between 1918 and 1920 Armenia experienced a brief period of independence, when some of the survivors took part in the founding of an independent Armenian republic, encompassing areas in the former Russian and Ottoman Empires. The Sovietization of Transcaucasia ended this precarious independence, and the imperial carve-up imposed by Moscow left the territories of Mountainous (Nagorno) Karabagh and Nakhichevan under the administration of the new Soviet Republic of Azerbaijan from the early 1920s. While Nakhichevan is today populated almost entirely by Azeris, Karabagh remains 75% Armenian in population.

Armenians have tried to redress the massive injustice of the genocide and to gain international recognition for their cause. From 1975 a minority resorted to violent means through terrorist activities, but subsequently Armenian organizations have used other, peaceful means, working through international bodies. This has lead to a recognition of the genocide by the UN Sub-Commission on the Prevention of Discrimination and the Protection of Minorities in 1986 and by the

Council of Europe in 1987. World attention returned to Soviet Armenia from the beginning of 1988, when the Karabagh issue again came to the fore. In the context of glasnost, Armenia, like the Baltic states, is demanding democratization – a process which encompasses the aspirations of the majority-Armenian population of Karabagh to be united with Armenia.

Whatever the other achievements of President Gorbachev, his initiatives on the subject of national and ethnic issues have been disappointingly feeble. At a time when the status of Karabagh could have been solved peacefully – by, for example, giving the city of Shushi, which is inhabited mainly by Azeris, to Azerbaijan in exchange for the corridor of territory which separates Karabagh from Armenia to Armenia – President Gorbachev, as in many other national problems, preferred to maintain a policy of 'divide and rule'.

The crisis came to a head in February 1988 when the Soviet of Mountainous Karabagh voted to demand the transfer of the territory to Armenia. Unfortunately the response of part of the Azeri population was a violent one: in Sumgait near Baku, anti-Armenian pogroms took place in February 1988, followed by further violence in Kirovabad in November 1988 and Baku in January 1990. A cycle of violence was set in motion. Armenians in Azerbaijan and Azeris in Armenia began a mass exodus, many fleeing to their national republics.

The anti-Armenian pogroms were not the actions of a majority of the Azeri population. But they make clear that the right to self-determination remains, even in the USSR today, a democratic prerogative which is denied to Soviet citizens. This book shows that it is the same struggle for recognition and self-determination which is the link between the genocide of 1915 and the events of the present.

**Gérard Chaliand**


Gérard Chaliand is a political scientist, an advisor to the Centre for Analysis and Planning for French Foreign Relations and the author of 20 books. He was President of the Groupement pour les Droits de Minorités (GDM, Paris) for 10 years. His family came from Armenia and he has continuing involvement with Armenia and its people.

## Acknowledgements

Parts of this book have previously been published under different titles. Chapters 1 to 7 were first published in a different order and format in *The Armenians*, by D.M. Lang and Christopher J. Walker (MRG, London, fifth edition, 1987). Chapters 8 to 14 were originally published in French as *Le Karabagh: une terre arménienne en Azerbaïdjan* by Patrick Donabédian and Claude Mutafian (GDM, Paris, 1988) and translated into English by Aline Werth. Material published in this book has been revised and updated to cover events until February 1991 by Christopher J. Walker, who acted as editor.

The transliterations of Armenian words used are those in common use in standard English language publications.

The opinions expressed in this book are those of the authors and editor. MRG gratefully thanks Gérard Chaliand for writing the Foreword to this book.

This book was produced by Kaye Stearman (Series Editor) Brian Morrison (Production Co-ordinator), Jacqueline Siapno (Editorial Assistant), Robert Webb (Publicity and Marketing Co-ordinator).

## About the authors

**Patrick Donabédian** wrote Chapter 9 and part of Chapter 10. He is an art historian specializing in the medieval art of Transcaucasia and is the author of a number of articles on the subject.

**David Marshall Lang** is, with Christopher J. Walker, responsible for Chapters 1 to 7. He was formerly Professor of Caucasian Studies at The School of Oriental and African Studies, London University and is the author of several books on Armenia.

**Claude Mutafian** wrote most of Chapter 10 and Chapters 11 to 14. He is a historian with a particular interest in the Near East and Armenia. and has written extensively on this area of study.

**Christopher J. Walker** acted as overall editor and co-author. He is a freelance writer and researcher specializing in Armenia its people and has written extensively on the subject.

# INTRODUCTION

The radical changes that have occurred in the USSR since 1985 have naturally brought changes to the situation in Armenia, the smallest of the Soviet republics. Following the introduction of perestroika, there was no immediate renewal; Armenia remained stagnant and Brezhnevite until 1987. Then the Communist Party structure began to shift, and eventually it crumbled altogether, but not under the weight of reform; rather it collapsed because of popular demands for the unification of Armenia with a neighbouring, largely Armenian-inhabited territory which is within the jurisdiction of Soviet Azerbaijan.

The near revolutionary situation that developed in Armenia in 1988 and 1989 related almost entirely to the struggle for this territory, known in Soviet parlance as the Nagorno Karabakh Autonomous *Oblast*, or NKAO for short. 'Nagorno Karabakh' (more correctly, Karabagh) means 'mountainous black garden'; *oblast* means 'region'. The population of this region, often known simply as Karabagh, or to give it its Armenian name, Artsakh, sought to end its association with Soviet Azerbaijan, to which it had been administratively assigned in 1923, and to unite it with Armenia, the republic with which its people shared language, cultural heritage and national identity.

These demands found a ready echo inside Armenia, and the popular mood there oscillated between great hopes, that perestroika would mean the ending of a 70-year-old injustice for the people of Karabagh, and bitter disappointment, that the Soviet state was, despite talk of change and renewal, unable or unwilling to make changes where they mattered most: on issues of nationality relating to the survival of national groups such as the Armenians of Nagorno Karabagh oppressed in alien, and often chauvinist, republics. Few nationalities had been so denied human rights and national identity as the Armenians of Nagorno Karabagh.

The struggle of the people of Karabagh, and of the parallel supporting struggle of the people of Armenia itself, is only one episode in the many struggles and tribulations of the Armenian people throughout

1

the last hundred years. However, other nations have also suffered bleak times. What makes the Armenian predicament different is that many of the bitterest experiences that they have been through are unknown, or to a great extent unacknowledged. In some cases, Armenian experiences are systematically denied by the enemies of Armenians, and by their client academics in some universities and places of higher education, as well as by professional political lobbyists in Washington, London and elsewhere, who have sometimes tried to conduct historical discourse through such media as advertisements in national newspapers.

Besides the Karabagh struggle, the main dispute of the Armenian people is with Turkey. It is not principally about territory or frontiers, or about Turkish treatment of the remaining Armenians within Turkey today, although these elements are nevertheless important; it is about what Turkey did to the Armenian population of what was then the Ottoman Empire at the time of World War I. Armenians, and most impartial students of the matter, claim that this amounted to a genocide, in the course of which about 1.5 million people died. It constituted a massive crime; it was an official attempt to liquidate the Armenian question by exterminating the Armenians. The measures had the further intention of facilitating the Turkish 'great idea' of pan-Turkism (that is, the political unity of all the Turkish-speaking peoples from the Balkans to Siberia). The Turks and their supporters vehemently oppose any talk of genocide; they claim that Armenian figures are exaggerated, and that the events of that time would be best characterized as a civil war between Armenians and Turks. Turks suffered from many harsh Armenian reprisals, they point out.

Although the Armenian question received widespread publicity from about 1894 to 1923 (when the Treaty of Lausanne effectively closed the issue in world diplomacy), thereafter there was virtual silence on the subject until 1965. It suited all parties to keep quiet. The Soviet government had no desire to permit expression of irredentist views within Soviet Armenia (except briefly in 1945); the Western world was happy to forget its statements of support for Armenians in its rush to support the modernization programme of Turkey's new dynamic leader, Mustafa Kemal (Ataturk). The half-million Armenian refugees were too busy living a hand-to-mouth existence in their adoptive countries to give any thought to mounting effective campaigns to redress their wrongs; and the Armenian political parties of the diaspora which led them were too absorbed in fighting amongst themselves to unite and press a broad claim against Turkey.

Some of this political and ideological landscape is, in the early

1990s, beginning to change. Since 1965 Armenian voices for recognition and even restitution have been heard more frequently. Turkey itself remains very sensitive on the subject of Armenians, even though the events in question took place before the foundation of the Turkish Republic. It prefers not to talk in non-propagandist terms about the issue, or else to publish volumes of pseudo-history and bizarre abuse about Armenians. Owing to the unfortunate predilection in a number of European and American universities for the Turkish version – an attitude which was built up in the years of the Cold War – such volumes, despite their abrogation of scholarly standards, sometimes receive a ready and serious response from academics.

Prejudice against Armenians in Western academic, and even diplomatic, circles was to some extent legitimized by the Cold War (when the attitude was to support Turkey whatever the cost); and despite the ending of the Cold War, a number of Western academics and ex-diplomats appear to remain quite 'Brezhnevite' in their incapacity or unwillingness to extend any understanding to the Armenian viewpoint, or to look seriously at its documentary basis. They continue to give almost uncritical support for the Turkish official version. As a result, much of what poses to be serious writing in academic journals about modern Armenian history is *parti pris*, selective and unreliable. It is Cold War, Nato history, which has an interest in cover-up and which does not seek to discover or explain the situation as it really was. Large amounts of important documentary evidence (especially German eyewitness dispatches of 1915) are simply overlooked by Ankara's clients.

Armenia's past history is indeed inextricably bound up with her present political situation. For no sooner has the USSR ceased to be the Cold War bogey of the West than semi-Independent Armenia, formerly the Armenian Soviet Socialist Republic (SSR), realized that its geographical situation, on the edge of an apparently disintegrating USSR, indicated that it might be in its interest to initiate commercial and diplomatic approaches with the Republic of Turkey. This makes some diplomatic and commercial sense, although an argument rages among Armenians about the risks attached to it. (It is always possible that Turkey will use such relations to impose dependency; and reports indicate that Turkey's price may be to insist on adhering to its ideological viewpoint about the Armenian genocide, that is, silence on the subject of the destruction of the Western Armenians, who lived in what is today eastern Turkey, which took place in 1915-16.) The Armenian government may indeed be compelled for economic reasons to moderate its attitude to its own history. This will only confirm what many have known for a long time: that it is not the business of governments of any hue to pronounce on history. Governments usually only produce statements which suit the present, and which are not accurate guides to the past.

In the decade before perestroika, before it became legitimate for the Armenian people to reclaim their own history, Armenian frustration at not having their case heard sometimes led to terrorism. Armenian activists claimed that the world had paid them no attention since 1915. This is only partially true. Armenians themselves put forward no serious, reasoned and accurate account of their sufferings and claims, using valid sources. Many Westerners were simply uninformed about Armenians, and there seemed to be no resource which could inform them. Recently, the Armenian case has been presented with greater persuasion and conviction, and the struggle within Armenia and Soviet Transcaucasia for Karabagh and for the reformation of the administration, has taken over as the central issue for Armenians. As a result, Armenian anti-Turkish terrorism has faded away and is no longer an issue.

In the 1980s, Armenian pressure groups made some headway with their cause – *Hai Tad* in Armenian – on four fronts. In the first place, the independent 'Permanent Peoples' Tribunal', composed of distinguished international jurists, meeting in Paris in 1984, found Turkey guilty of genocide 'according to the Convention of 9 December 1948'. (The proceedings and verdict of the Tribunal have been published; see Select Bibliography). Secondly, Armenians in the United States are pressing for a House Joint Resolution to be adopted by Congress. This resolution seeks to declare 24 April, the day on which Armenians worldwide commemorate the genocide of 1915, a US national day of remembrance of 'man's inhumanity to man'. The move is being vigorously opposed by the Turkish government and its agencies.

Thirdly, a report was prepared in 1987 by Mr. Ben Whitaker, former director of the Minority Rights Group, in his capacity of Special Rapporteur on Genocide, for the United Nations Sub-Commission on the Prevention of Discrimination and Protection of Minorities which meets annually in Geneva, which, in the course of proposing reforms of the 1948 UN Convention on Genocide, cited the Turkish extermination of Armenians of 1915 as an example of the crime. And fourthly, the Political Committee of the European Parliament at Strasbourg has decided that the Armenian question is a fit matter for the European Assembly to concern itself with.

None of these measures have as yet led to any significant growth in public awareness of the Armenian situation, or to a belief that Armenia is a legitimate subject for international political discourse; yet they are not without significance. But if real change is to come to the Armenian situation, it will most probably come from Yerevan and from Karabagh, not from Western pressure groups and resolutions.

This book, parts of which were originally written for a report by the Minority Rights Group, first issued in 1976 with its fifth edition in 1987, focuses on an account of recent developments within the Armenian community, and Turkish attitudes to the Armenian question. However, the emphasis remains on casting the cold eye of historical and archaeological research on the – in the words of the 1976 report – 'elaborate and quite fanciful ideas that the Turks (who, of course, settled in Turkey from Central Asia some ten centuries ago) are really the original inhabitants of Armenia and Asia Minor'. In addition this book gives a detailed account of the history and background to the present conflict in Mountainous Karabagh and its attempts to reunify with the newly renamed Republic of Armenia, which is itself working towards some sort of self-determination, whether inside or outside the USSR

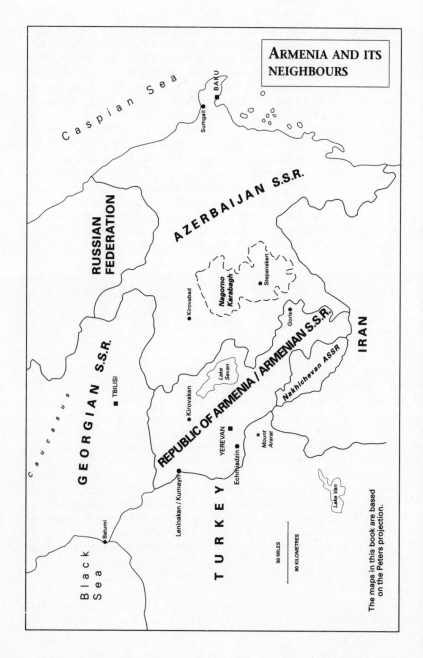

ARMENIA AND ITS NEIGHBOURS

Caspian Sea

BAKU

Sumgait

RUSSIAN FEDERATION

AZERBAIJAN S.S.R.

Kirovabad

*Nagorno Karabagh*

Stepanakert

Goris

IRAN

GEORGIAN S.S.R.

*Lake Sevan*

Kirovakan

REPUBLIC OF ARMENIA / ARMENIAN S.S.R.

*Nakhichevan ASSR*

TBILISI

C a u c a s u s

★ Mount Ararat

YEREVAN

Echmiadzin

Leninakan / Kumayri

Batumi

TURKEY

*Lake Van*

Black Sea

50 MILES

80 KILOMETRES

The maps in this book are based on the Peters projection.

6

# 1

# THE ARMENIAN PEOPLE

## The land

The Armenian homeland, known historically as Great Armenia, comprises a large area of mountainous country. If we take the western boundary as situated between Kharput and Malatya in Turkey, and the eastern boundary between Khoi in Persian Azerbaijan, and the Soviet Karabagh, this makes a distance of over 720 km. (450 miles) 'as the crow flies'. From Armenia's northern border between Ardahan and Lake Sevan, southwards to the traditional frontier with Kurdistan, below Lake Van, measures some 400 km. (250 miles). Allowing for the country's irregular shape, we arrive at an area of not less than 260,000 sq. km. (100,000 sq. miles).

The revised *Encyclopaedia of Islam* includes within 'historical Armenia' – the *Arminiyya* of the Arab Abbasid geographers – much of present-day Kurdistan, including the Hakkiari country. According to that authority, Great Armenia takes in all land between longitudes 37 and 49 East, and latitudes 37.5 and 41.5 North. This encyclopedia estimates a total area for Arminiyya of about 300,000 sq. km. (115,800 sq. miles).

Lesser Armenia during the medieval period was a district of northwestern Armenia, adjoining what is now the Turkish-Kurdish city of Erzinjan. From the 11th to the 14th Centuries, there existed an important Armenian kingdom in Cilicia, north of the Gulf of Alexandretta, and including St. Paul's birthplace of Tarsus and the modern city of Adana. This kingdom was ruled by the Armenian dynasty of the Rupenids, and then by the French Lusignans. It fell to the Mamluks of Egypt in 1375. Cilicia is also known as 'Little Armenia'.

Soviet Armenia today takes in only 10% of the territory of ancient Great Armenia, comprising 29,800 sq. km. (11,500 sq. miles). Within the USSR, several Armenian ethnic areas are enclosed as enclaves within the Azerbaijan Socialist Soviet Republic (SSR), the most important one being the Mountainous Karabagh, which still has a population which is 75% Armenian.

Modern maps of Turkey exclude all mention of Armenia. The area once known as 'Turkish Armenia' is now shown as being unquestionably part of Turkey, and many Armenian place names have been replaced by Turkish forms. All mention of 'Turkish Armenia' is prohibited.

Parts of Armenia, notably the River Araxes valley, and the Van district, are fertile and beautiful. However, this is true of less than a quarter of Armenia's overall territory. Far from being a 'land of milk and honey', the larger part of Armenia is virtually uninhabitable. The landscape is cut up by enormous mountains, many being extinct volcanoes over 2600 metres (10,000 feet) high. Armenia's highest peak, Mount Ararat, rises to almost 5200 metres (17,000 feet). The average height of the Armenian plateau is over 1666 metres (5000 feet). This windswept region has a harsh climate, winter continuing for seven months, and the short, dry summer being only three months long. A typical Armenian town, such as Leninakan (recently named Kumayri), on the Soviet/Turkish border, stands 1638 metres (5078 feet) above sea level, and has an average winter temperature of -11 C. Armenia is often shaken by destructive earthquakes. The Varto area and adjoining regions west of Lake Van were severely affected during the 1970s, while the earthquake of December 1988 led to widespread death and destruction in and around Leninakan.

Transport is poor throughout much of the area. There are few navigable rivers, though boats can sail on Lakes Van and Sevan. Recently, a rail link between Istanbul and Tehran has been established, via Lake Van, and the trunk road between Tabriz and Erzerum has been improved for heavy lorries and bus traffic. The transport situation is most developed in Soviet Armenia. Direct air service by Aeroflot links Yerevan with Moscow and there is also direct contact with Tbilisi, Leningrad, other Soviet cities and even with Paris, Aleppo, and, at times, Beirut. Mainline railway services exist between Yerevan and Baku, and Yerevan and Tbilisi, and thence to other parts of the USSR. However, the road blockade of 1990 through Azerbaijan has disrupted normal services and caused great hardships.

Armenia is quite rich in precious and semi-precious metals and minerals. However, there is no oil. In Soviet Armenia, progress has been made in harnessing the waters of the River Razdan (or Hrazdan) for hydro-electric schemes.

A particularly hard fact of geography is Great Armenia's lack of access to the sea. Being cut off from Russia by the main Caucasus range, Armenia's nearest maritime outlets are such ports as Trebizond in Turkey, Batumi in Georgia, and Baku in Azerbaijan. From 1080 to

1375 AD, the Cilician kingdom of Armenia had direct access to the eastern Mediterranean through several excellent ports, but this was only temporary. Otherwise Armenia is entirely landlocked and has always suffered from this fact both economically and politically.

## The people

Although they speak an Indo-European language, the Armenians are descended from ancient tribes who inhabited their traditional homeland in Eastern Anatolia since prehistoric times. There is a remarkable archaeological record of continuous human occupation of the region around Mount Ararat, since the Old Stone Age. To this extent, the Biblical legend of Noah's Ark reflects historical reality, especially as a number of animals and birds, and useful plants, have developed from prototypes still extant in Transcaucasia.

Before 1000 BC, Armenia became dominated by a people known as the Urartians. 'Urartu' is actually the same name as Ararat, in the Assyrian language. The Urartians founded an important kingdom, based on the city of Van, where their ruined palaces and castles exist even today. Around 600 BC, Urartu was overrun by various invaders, among whom were the Scythians, the Medes (ancestors of the present-day Kurds), and some people calling themselves 'Hayasa', who came from Central Anatolia, close to the old Hittite state. The Armenians of today call their land Hayastan, and their legendary ancestor, Haik. The ancient inhabitants of Armenia/Urartu did not die out, but became mingled with these invading elements. Though retaining much of their old ethnic identity, they adopted a new language, which is a distinctive member of the Indo-European group.

Persian and Greek sources begin to speak of 'Armina' and 'Armenians' from about 500 BC. They were known under these names to the great kings Darius and Xerxes of Persia, and to the 'Father of History', Herodotus. This attests to continuous occupation by the Armenian nation of the land known as 'Great Armenia' and adjoining districts, from well before 500 BC until the annihilation of virtually all the community living in eastern Turkey in 1915, amounting to an uninterrupted period of two and a half thousand years.

Today the scattered Armenians number at least six million, spread virtually all around the world. As a community they are marked by success in business and professional life: university lecturers, scientists, mathematicians, doctors and dentists. They excel in the arts and in literature and are numbered among orchestral conductors and soloists, film directors, sculptors and book illustrators. Armenians are noted for their humour, in spite of their tragic history, and many political jokes in the USSR are ascribed to a mythical Radio Yerevan.

## How many Armenians?

The Armenians are a mobile, as well as being a widely scattered people, so it has always been hard to establish the total world population of Armenians at any given time. Estimates – even seemingly reliable ones – vary widely.

The Armenian Apostolic Church plays a central role in the life of the community; many Armenians regard membership of the Church as an essential and integral part of 'being an Armenian'. According to Patriarch Ormanian's history of the Armenian Church, Apostolic Church members immediately before the World War I numbered 3,472,000 all over the world. In addition there were 128,400 Roman Catholic Armenians, and 49,000 Protestant ones. Allowing for persons of Armenian origin not recorded as members of any church, it is reasonable to estimate a 1914 world Armenian population of about four and a half million, of whom a million and a half perished in the Turkish genocide of 1915 and its aftermath. A world-wide low point of three million was reached during the famine years of 1918 to 1920.

There has been the systematic build-up of the population of Soviet Armenia, particularly since 1945. In 1954, Bishop Poladian calculated that there were 2,745,000 Armenians living within the USSR as a whole. Due to political and social discrimination by the Ataturk regime and its successors, the Armenian population of Turkey was in 1954 still at its immediate post-genocide level of around 100,000. Even in the 1990s, there is still no Armenian resettlement of the area formerly known as Turkish Armenia.

The world upward trend was further confirmed by the break-down given in 1966 by the Yerevan periodical *Hayreniki Dzayn*.[1] This gives a world total of five and a half million Armenians, divided between the USSR and diaspora.

### Armenian Population est. 1966

| | |
|---|---|
| USSR | 3,500,000 |
| Rest of the world | 2,000,000 |

The Soviet Armenian community was classified as follows:

| | |
|---|---|
| Armenian SSR | 2,000,000 |
| Azerbaijan SSR | 560,000 |
| Georgian SSR | 550,000 |
| Russian RSFSR | 330,000 |
| Others | 60,000 |
| **Total** | **3,500,000** |
| (1979 *Soviet census* total | 4,151,241) |

| | |
|---|---|
| USA/Canada | 450,000 |
| Turkey | 250,000 |
| Iran | 200,000 |
| France | 200,000 |
| Lebanon | 180,000 |
| Syria | 150,000 |
| Others | 570,000 |
| **Total** | **2,000,000** |

'Others' includes countries such as the UK (about 6000), Germany, Italy, Austria, Switzerland, Bulgaria (about 25,000), Romania, Poland, Cyprus, Egypt, South America, India, Burma, Singapore, China, and Australia. The inflated figure of 250,000 for Turkey is suspect, and must include many 'camouflaged' Armenians who have taken Turkish names and adopted Islam to avoid persecution. With marked exuberance, an Armenian magazine published in Vienna in July 1975 declared: 'Ils sont sept millions dans le monde qui disent ayo!' ('Seven million people in the world say "ayo"!' – 'Ayo' being the Armenian for 'yes'.) According to this source, there were today as many as 350,000 Armenians in France alone.

Official Soviet statistics estimated the population of Soviet Armenia at 3,317,000 (1985 figures), of which a total of almost three million were Armenians. It is, however, noticeable that the birth-rate in Soviet Armenia has shown a significant decrease since the peak year of 1958, when it reached 41.1 per 1000 inhabitants, as against 8.1 deaths per 1000, leaving a net growth rate of 33 per 1000. By 1984 the growth rate had sunk to 18.4 per 1000. This compares with a rapid 28.4 per 1000 among the Muslim Tajiks, and a sparse 4.0 per 1000 among the Estonians. Deportation and emigration are also matters to be dealt with. Nearly 10,000 Soviet Armenians emigrated to the USA during 1975-80 while there was also immigration from abroad, varying according to Soviet government policy.

**Their religion**

During the long years of Armenia's subjection to foreign empires, the national Apostolic Church was the one factor which kept the national spirit alive, even if it was dormant. By the late 19th Century, the Church had come to be recognized as a vehicle of nationalism and self-defence within the empires. It was through the Church that Armenian leaders sought to educate their people, and imperial functionaries (especially Turkish ones) were not slow to discover that education was dangerous.

Besides the adherents of the Armenian Apostolic Church, there were a number of Armenian Uniate Catholics, some dating from the time of the Crusades and others from later Dominican missionary activity. In the 18th Century their patriarchate moved from Aleppo, where there had been disturbances between them and adherents of the Armenian Apostolic Church, to Bzommar in Mount Lebanon, which is situated in land belonging to the powerful Maronite Khazen family. Armenian Protestants dated from the period of American missionary activity (1830s onwards) and by the middle of the century were an officially recognized community within the Ottoman Empire.

In the period of the persecutions of the 1890s, adherents of the 'national' Church were singled out for especially harsh treatment. This was partly because the Church, as the guardian of the people, was inevitably being forced into a more political role as persecution increased, and partly because the Ottoman government understood that it would encounter no diplomatic response if it attacked Gregorian Armenians, whereas if Armenian Catholics were attacked, the French (or Austro-Hungarian) ambassador would protest, and if Protestants were attacked, the British or Americans would make their voices heard. During the Young Turk genocide of 1915 such distinctions were ignored, and Armenians regardless of religious adherence were killed.

The problems of the Church after the establishment of Communist rule in Armenia were immense, and for long periods the Catholicosate of Echmiadzin was left vacant. The Cilician catholicosate (which in theory had similar powers, while recognizing that the title of the Echmiadzin catholicos was 'Catholicos of all Armenians') moved after the World War I to Antilias, north of Beirut, where it continues to exist today. After its reconstitution in 1929, the Cilician catholicosate comprised the bishoprics of Aleppo, Damascus, Beirut and Cyprus. In 1956, it adopted a new constitution which permits it to appoint bishops in regions previously under the jurisdiction of Echmiadzin. It now has responsibility for additional dioceses in Iran, Greece, Kuwait, and parts of the USA and Canada.

A split in the Armenian Church began in 1933 and was formalized in 1956. Since then, various attempts have been made to heal it since it also adds up to a split in the community. What has, if anything, brought the different wings together, and gone some way to creating an atmosphere for reconciliation within the church, was the struggle over Mountainous Karabagh, and the tragedy of the 1988 earthquake. Both catholicoses are now working in harmony together.

The international standing of the Armenian Apostolic Church was enhanced by the official visit of the then Archbishop of Canterbury, Dr. Donald Coggan, to Echmiadzin early in October 1977. Armenian prelates from all over the world gathered there to welcome the first primate of the Anglican Church ever to visit Armenia. British press reports expressed amazement at the large crowds, including many young people, who assembled for the occasion, and commented that expression of religious enthusiasm was freer in Armenia than in other Soviet republics which the British delegation had visited.

The present Catholicos of Cilicia, Karekin II, is a man of broad outlook, whose Oxford thesis was published by Society for Propagation of Christian Knowledge (SPCK) as *The Council of Chalcedon and the Armenian Church*. He was instrumental in laying the foundation stone for an Armenian church at Deir ez-Zor, where hundreds of thousands of Armenians perished in a concentration camp in 1915.

# 2

## ARMENIA AND ITS HISTORY

### Ancient Armenia

Armenians are understandably proud of the fact that their country was once a great power – though only for a couple of generations, in the time of Pompey and Julius Caesar. The greatest Armenian king was called Tigranes II, and he ruled from 95 to 55 BC. His realm extended from the Caspian Sea right across the Middle East to Syria and the Mediterranean Sea. However, Tigranes was conquered by the Roman general Lucullus – inventor of the Lucullan banquet, financed by Armenian gold. Further defeats were inflicted on the Armenians by Pompey. It is worth noting that Tigranes' son, King Artavazd II, was a man of outstanding literary culture, who composed plays in Greek, and founded a Greek theatre at his court in Armenia. Artavazd fell foul of Antony and Cleopatra, who kidnapped Artavazd and his family and put them to death.

If we except the now vanished Christian realm of King Abgar of Edessa, Armenia is the oldest Christian nation in the world. The introduction of Christianity is ascribed to St. Gregory the Illuminator who, after torture and rejection, later converted the pagan Armenian sovereign Tiridates III, probably in the year 301 AD. Christianity developed in Armenia independently of Rome and Constantinople. There are therefore certain doctrinal and liturgical differences. But this does not affect the Armenian church's claim to represent an authentic apostolic tradition in the Near East.

The distinctive Armenian alphabet was invented early in the 5th Century AD, by St. Mesrop Mashtots. Previously, all literature and official documents had been written down in Greek or in Middle Iranian. This invention of a national script enabled the Bible and most of the important works of early Christian literature to be translated into Armenian.

The establishment of a national church proved of vital importance in preserving Armenian national unity. Such were the political pressures that without their church the Armenians would long ago have

15

been assimilated by their neighbours. A fateful political decision was taken in 387 AD, when the Romans and Persians carved up Armenia between them. In 428, the last king of the Armeno-Parthian dynasty of the Arsacids died, and was not replaced. Feudal barons or nakharars vied for supreme power. The Persian Zoroastrian king Yezdegird did everything possible to suppress Christianity, invading Armenia in 451 with an enormous army, including squadrons of elephants. Persian domination was later followed by that of the Arab caliphs, who sent their generals (including one named Bogha the Turk) to ravage the land.

## Medieval Armenia

The Byzantine emperors also treated Armenia in a domineering manner. They deported thousands of Armenians into Thrace and Macedonia. However, several Byzantine emperors were themselves Armenians. These include remarkable Basil I (867-886) and the able but unpopular Leo the Armenian (813-820). Another Armenian emperor was John Tzimiskes (969-976), one of the most brilliant conquerors ever to sit on the throne in Constantinople. During the 9th Century, the Armenian monarchy was restored under the dynasty of the Bagratids, whose capital (now in ruins) can still be seen at Ani, on the frontier between Turkey and Soviet Armenia. Another Armenian dynasty existed in the province of Vaspurakan, further south. One of its rulers, King Gagik, built the famous church of Aghtamar, on an island in Lake Van. The revival of the Armenian independent monarchy proved short-lived. In 1045 the Byzantines annexed Ani and abolished the monarchy of the Bagratids. The Seljuq Turks soon swept in from central Asia and Iran, and overran Ani and much of Anatolia in 1064.

Armenian emigration from the homeland grew into a flood. The Armenians were successful in founding a new kingdom in Cilicia (1080-1375), with its capital at Sis. There they became allies of the Crusaders, and the last king of Cilician Armenia, Levon V Lusignan, died in exile in Paris in 1393. A number of Armenians crossed the Black Sea to found trading colonies in the Crimea. Thence they spread into Russia, Romania and Poland. Armenians played an important role in building up the Moldavian state of Prince Alexander the Good (1401-1435), while the ruler John the Brave of Moldavia (1572-1574) was himself an Armenian. In Poland, Armenians were prominent in the commercial and intellectual life of Cracow and Lvov; in the latter city, they built a fine cathedral which has recently been well restored.

Within a century of the fall of Constantinople to the Turks in 1453, the Ottoman frontier was established with the empire's eastern neighbour (initially Iran, later Russia), a frontier which persists to this day. Like Poland, Armenia was doomed to have her land divided among other people's empires. Within Ottoman Turkey, the Armenians were organized into their own semi-autonomous community or *millet*, with the Armenian Patriarch of Constantinople at its head. (However, recent research seems to show that his authority was less absolute than previously believed.)

Over the centuries, the community came to be dominated by an elite of merchants and high officials; and until a period of internal reform in the 18th Century, the Patriarchate was often seen as an office to be sold to the highest bidder, with its attendant corruption. In the wealthy environment of Constantinople, Armenians and Turks developed a remarkable understanding of one another, and Armenians served the empire well as bankers, heads of government concerns and imperial architects. Until the emergence of national sentiment in the late 19th Century, Ottoman Armenians were known as the 'loyal *millet*'.

Early in the 17th Century, Shah Abbas the Great of Persia deported thousands of Armenians, mostly from the plain of Ararat, to his capital at Isfahan. There they founded a colony at New Julfa, with a cathedral and several fine churches. For 100 years they prospered in Persia. Then, as conditions became unstable, from Persia they spread into Russia, India, Burma, Singapore, Java, and more recently, into Australia.

**The Nineteenth Century: Armenians in Ottoman Turkey**

Within the Ottoman Empire, Armenians formed four broad classes. The first consisted of the rich and influential men in the government and civil service. The second was the mercantile and trading class of Istanbul and the cities of Anatolia; this was the class with which Western travellers came into most contact. The third class was the peasantry – much the largest of the four and the least regarded, except by a few knowledgeable travellers such as H.F.B. Lynch. The fourth was the warrior class of the mountaineers – men living a tough, independent existence in remote mountain fastnesses like Zeitun. In addition, there was a numerous priesthood and higher clergy.

How many Armenians were there in Turkey? There were no reliable independent population statistics. Ubicini (1854) put the figure at 2.4 million, and held that they constituted a majority in the provinces of Erzerum (which then included Kars, Bayazid and Childer) and Kurdistan (Van, Moush, Hakkiari and Diyarbakir). In 1882 the Armenian

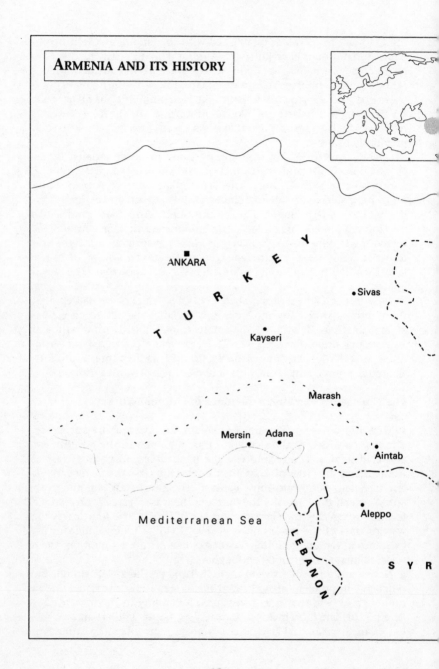

ARMENIA AND ITS HISTORY

ANKARA

TURKEY

Sivas

Kayseri

Marash

Mersin    Adana

Aintab

Aleppo

Mediterranean Sea

LEBANON

SYR

50 MILES

80 KILOMETRES

| | |
|---|---|
| —·—·—·— | Present-day National Boundaries |
| — — — — | Historic Armenia |
| — · — · — · | Cilicia (1080 – 1375) |
| ·············· | Extension of pre-Soviet Independent Armenia (1918 – 20) |
| — — — — | Wilson's proposed boundaries (1920) |

patriarchate in Constantinople produced figures estimating Armenians in the Empire at 2.66 million, of whom 1.63 million lived in the 'six [Armenian] *vilayets*' – the provinces of Sivas, Mamuret el-Aziz, Erzerum, Diyarbakir, Bitlis and Van. Later statistics from the patriarchate in 1912 put the total at only 2.1 million; the decrease was due to the massacres of the 1890s, and the continual shift of the Armenian population across the frontier into the Russian Caucasus. Official Turkish figures put the Armenian population considerably lower.

The Ottoman Turkish government had exercised little direct authority over the majority of its Armenian citizens until the second half of the 19th Century. Up to that date, the majority in the country areas were beholden to local Kurdish feudal lords. When central government encroached, the result was almost always bad: it meant extra taxes for the peasantry, and an increase in oppression. The Armenians in 'Turkish Armenia' (that is, eastern Turkey of today) had an additional problem to cope with. They were heavily intermixed with a large Kurdish population. These Kurds, originally from more southerly regions, had been settled there by Sultan Selim in the 16th Century, on condition that they guard the frontier with Persia. The Kurds are mostly orthodox Muslims. Though not fanatical, their tendencies for pillaging, and for stealing Armenian girls, were strong. Moreover the Kurds were armed, whereas the Armenians, as a Christian subject race, were forbidden to bear arms.

Slowly the Armenians were squeezed out. In 1839, Consul Brant had reported that 'in the whole plain of Moush there are not any Mohammedan peasants intermingled with the Armenians', but within a few decades, they were a minority in their own land. The Armenian peasantry was sometimes heavily indebted to the Kurds, who acted as money-lenders, and charged a rate of interest of between 3% and 4% per month.

The reform movements of the 19th Century in Ottoman Turkey, known as the 'Tanzimat' or reorganization, hardly benefited the Armenians at all outside Constantinople, the main reason being that the civil administration of the empire was not reorganized. And it is arguable that the 'Tanzimat' was little but a piece of window dressing, designed to pacify European diplomats pressing the 'sick man of Europe' towards some semblance of reform.

## Armenia and the Great Powers

Armenia did not feature as an issue in international diplomacy until 1878. Her people were not rebellious, so European diplomats tended to overlook them. But the education that Armenians were receiving, whether in France, Venice or Russia, meant that the old subservience would not last. Moreover, the capture of eastern Armenia by the Russians from the Persians in 1828, and their creation there of an 'Armenian province', gave a boost to nationalist sentiment. However, Russian rule was rather more repressive than the somewhat over-hopeful Armenians anticipated, and in many ways was little improvement on the Persian administration; although Russia contained within itself the seeds of modernization, which Qajar Iran did not.

With the Treaty of Paris (1856), Ottoman Turkey was first admitted as a treaty partner with the great powers; and entry into the 'club' was secured through Article 9 of that treaty, which promised amelioration for the Christian population of the empire. At the time the European powers were thinking not of the Armenians but of the Balkan Christians; however, there was no distinction between Balkan and Armenian in the treaty itself. No substantial reforms were made, except for Armenians in the imperial capital; conditions in the provinces continued as they had always been.

At the same time it was a period of 'exchange of populations', exacerbating distinctions of race and religion. Tens of thousands of Armenians fled to eastern Armenia following its Russian conquest in 1828; and following the Crimean War and the Russian subjugation of Circassia, hundreds of thousands of Muslims fled to the Ottoman Empire. Russia moved on to subdue Central Asia, where the fate of rebellious or disaffected Muslims was frequently death. These things increased rather than diminished racial and religious animosity.

Nevertheless Armenians continued to hope that the administration of their people in the Ottoman provinces would improve. At this stage Armenians were seeking reforms in the administration, not independence; it was not until after World War I did any of them, except a small unrepresentative group of revolutionaries, seek independence. Armenian hopes were highest after the Russo-Turkish war of 1877-78; by this time they had grown in self-awareness, and knew that their people deserved better than to be treated as serfs by the local Turks and Kurds.

But the hopes of the Armenians were frustrated, largely by the British Prime Minister, Disraeli. He viewed the introduction of reforms in the Ottoman Empire merely as an advance in Russian power, which was unacceptable. Disraeli and Lord Salisbury forced the Russians to evacuate Erzerum, although they were allowed to keep Kars and Ardahan. An unworkable clause was introduced into the Treaty of Berlin (1878), laying the Western powers under an obscure collective obligation to check on Turkey's introduction of administrative reforms; the upshot was that 'What was everybody's business became nobody's business', as the Duke of Argyll was later to observe. Half a dozen British consuls were left with the impossible task of policing – without any real powers of coercion – an area the size of England and Wales; and they were ordered home after four years. Disraeli, however, cleverly wrested Cyprus from the Turkish sultan, as the price for a defence treaty with Britain.

Britain's guilt in leaving the Armenians unprotected was later recognized by Lloyd George; he noted in 1938 that, in the Treaty of Berlin, which was 'entirely due to our minatory pressure' and which 'was acclaimed by us as a great British triumph which brought peace with honour', 'Armenia was sacrificed on the triumphal altar we had erected. The Russians were forced to withdraw; the wretched Armenians were once more placed under the heel of their old masters . . .' However, despite these high sentiments, it should be pointed out that during his premiership in 1918 to 1920, Lloyd George did as little for the Armenians as any of his predecessors. He exhibited the fatal tendency of the British to wring their hands at the fate of Armenians but do nothing concrete in their behalf.

Bit by bit Britain lost its position of predominance at the court of the sultan. Reforms were never introduced into Turkish Armenia. And the Turkish court gravitated more and more towards the German capital at Berlin, where Bismarck and later Kaiser Wilhelm II were proclaiming that 'Might is Right'.

# 3

# THE ERA OF MASSACRES

In the course of quarter of a century – between 1895 and 1920 – the Armenian nation lost a million and a half persons by the gun or the bayonet, by deliberate starvation, and by privation and disease. About a third of all Armenians in the world died a gruesome, painful death. This national catastrophe is comparable to that suffered by the Jews under the Hitler regime. No Armenian household today, in the 1990s, is free of memories of this holocaust. It is referred to constantly in the Armenian press, and seems set to become more of a live issue in years to come.

## The Armenian Revolutionary Movement

Though life continued to be tolerable, even enviable, for the wealthy Armenians of the great cities of the Ottoman Empire, the situation in the eastern provinces went from bad to worse. Instead of the administration being reformed, oppression by local officials grew more intense. Abdul Hamid armed the Kurds, and encouraged them to attack the Armenian villagers. In 1891 he established the Kurdish Hamidiye regiments, which terrorized the civilian population, just as Cossack troops in Russia did during the final years of Tsarism.

The Armenians for their part began to form underground defence groups and armed revolutionary societies. The first of these were the Armenakans of Van (1885), followed by the Hunchaks (1887, founded in Geneva) and the Dashnaks (1890, Tiflis). The last two were revolutionary socialist groups, drawing their inspiration from Russian committees like the *Narodnaya Volya*. The Dashnaks often used armed threats against rich and conservative Armenians who refused to support the cause: they claimed, with some justification, that the regimes they opposed were more brutal and terroristic to the mass of their people than their own intimidation. However, the split which opened within the Armenian community between conservatives and gradualists on one side, and radicals and party authoritarians on the other side, was to have serious and lasting implications.

During the early 1890s, these groups carried out a few acts of armed defiance of the Turkish authorities, and put up seditious placards calling on the people to revolt. But the first really significant action was the attempt by Hunchaks in 1894 to incite the Armenians of Sasun in Turkish Armenia to defy both the Ottoman government and their local Kurdish overlords. The two leading revolutionaries, Mihran Damadian and Hampartzum Boyadjian, were, respectively, a teacher and a doctor.

## Sultan Abdul Hamid and the 1894-96 massacres

The Sasun rising was suppressed with considerable ferocity by Ottoman regulars, which led to an international outcry. Foreign pressure forced the sultan to appoint a commission, with delegates from Britain, France and Russia as observers. Abdul Hamid promised reforms, but there followed in October-December 1895 a series of massacres throughout Turkish Armenia, in almost every one of which, impartial observers, including British consuls, noted official complicity. Just before these killings took place, the Hunchaks had organized a large and violent demonstration in Istanbul, which served as an additional pretext for the authorities to slaughter the Armenian populace.

In these massacres, up to 300,000 Armenians perished. One of the worst was the second massacre at Urfa on 28-29 December 1895. About 3000 Armenian men, women and children had taken refuge in their cathedral, but troops soon broke in. After shooting down many unarmed victims, the Turks collected straw bedding, poured kerosene on it, and set it alight. British Consul Fitzmaurice later wrote:

> *'The gallery beams and wooden framework soon caught fire, whereupon, blocking up the staircase leading to the gallery with similar inflammable materials, they left the mass of struggling human beings to become the prey of the flames. During several hours the sickening odour of roasting flesh pervaded the town, and even today, two months and a half after the massacre, the smell of putrescent and charred remains in the church is unbearable.'*

In despair, the Armenian revolutionaries resolved to force intervention by the European powers who had signed the Treaty of Berlin of 1878. In August 1896, a group of armed Dashnaks seized the Ottoman Bank in Constantinople, and threatened to blow it up unless their political demands were met. But they surrendered after holding the Bank for 13 hours; all they obtained was free passage out of the country. However, they were the lucky ones; as they left, the sultan organized another massacre of Armenians on the streets of the capital, despite the presence of the foreign ambassadors there. Most of those killed were Armenians of the poorest class – migrant workers, porters, dockers and caretakers.

Pressed by Gladstone and others to intervene, Lord Salisbury commented that, unfortunately, British battleships could not operate over the Taurus mountains. The European powers discussed the possible partition of the Ottoman Empire, or even the forcible deposition of Sultan Abdul Hamid. But their mutual rivalries and mistrust, and the enormous sums invested by some of them in the economy of the Ottoman Empire, prevented any effective action being taken. There is no doubt that the sultan was responsible for giving orders to kill Armenians; yet, absurdly, some Western academics disregard the most significant diplomatic dispatches, and attempt to prove that the sultan, and not the Armenian peasantry, was the victim.

## A false dawn: Armenia and the Young Turk revolution

The Young Turk revolution of 1908 removed the autocratic powers of Sultan Abdul Hamid and reintroduced the Constitution of 1876. Initially there was a tremendous sense of liberty and fraternity among the nationalities within the Empire; Armenian Dashnaks had collaborated closely with the Young Turks in staging the revolution, and maintained an alliance with them for a few years thereafter. Few Ottoman Armenians were crude and jingoistic Armenian nationalists. All saw the importance of preserving a connection with other peoples of the Ottoman administration.

Yet even within one year, relations turned rather sour. In 1909 there was a huge massacre of Armenians in Adana, claiming about 30,000 victims. It is not clear whether the Young Turks, or partisans of the deposed Abdul Hamid, were behind this violent episode. Soon the Young Turk revolution was degenerating into dictatorship, and the policy of the ruling junta became one of 'the Turks above all other nationalities'. The British Ambassador described the junta's policy in September 1910 as, 'pounding the non-Turkish elements in a Turkish mortar' – a remark which applies equally well to the Turkish government in the late 20th Century.

At the same time, a Turkish nationalist ideology was taking shape which was to have grave and far-reaching implications for the Armenians. This was pan-Turkism or pan-Turanianism – a doctrine which continues even today to have many powerful adepts in Turkish ruling circles. Serge Zenkovsky describes the ideology thus:

*'First, the Ottoman Turks had to consolidate their grip over their empire and Turkicize its minorities. In the second, 'pan-Turkic', phase, the closest relatives of the Ottoman Turks – the Azerbaijanis of Russia and Persia (the south-eastern group of Turkic peoples) – were to be taken into the Turkic state. The third step would be the uniting of all the Turanian peoples of Asia around the Turkish core.'*

A biographer of one of the chief pan-Turkists, Zia Gokalp, comments:

*'Gokalp, Halide Edib and their associates dreamt of a union of all the Turks under a single ruler who would renew the days of Attila, Jengiz Khan or Timur-leng.'*

The implications of pan-Turkism for the Armenians were extremely grave. They were among the least willing of the minorities within the empire to be Turkicized, clinging to their ancient church as a symbol of that defiance. Moreover, their fellow Armenians in the Russian Caucasus stood in the way of the 'second stage' of pan-Turkism – the expansion to Baku, the oil city on the Caspian.

This theorizing was far from being harmless, intellectual speculation – any more than the Aryan myth was under the regime of Adolf Hitler. By 1914 Ottoman Turkey was ruled by a triumvirate of Young Turk militants, and pan-Turkism was the personal ideology of the most powerful of the three, Enver Pasha. The second of the trio, Talaat, was less of a theoretician, but capable of crushing the minority nationalities, and with an abundance of bureaucratic cruelty in his character. The third, Jemal, was of a relatively affable disposition, but with more than a streak of ruthlessness.

## World War I and the 'final solution' of the Armenian question

It is often stated by Turkish historians that the mass deportation of the Armenians was forced on the Young Turk government of that time, because the entire Armenian population constituted a dangerous 'Fifth Column', sympathetic to the Western Allies and to Russia. This claim is less than the whole truth. Just two years before, Armenians had fought bravely in the Ottoman army during the Balkan War; the British ambassador had remarked that 'the several thousand of Armenian troops have fought better than any of the other non-Turkish elements'. In 1914, there were a number of professions of Armenian loyalty to the Ottoman Empire (notably the enlistment of Armenians in the Ottoman army); however, the previous 40 years had taught the

Armenians to be wary of any Turkish government, none of which had shown evidence of being their government.

Shortly before World War I broke out in 1914, the Dashnak party held its eighth party conference in Erzerum. During the conference, Young Turk representatives approached the Dashnaks and suggested that they should foment a rebellion across the frontier, in the Russian Caucasus. In return, Turkey would set up an autonomous Armenia under her own protection. The Dashnaks turned down the plan, proposing instead that Turkey should stay neutral in the impending conflict; but in the event of Turkey joining the war, Armenians everywhere would be advised to do their duty as Ottoman citizens.

When war broke out, most Turkish Armenians behaved as loyal Ottoman citizens. An estimated 60,000 were conscripted into the Ottoman armies. When Enver Pasha was defeated by the Russians at Sarikamish in January 1915, it was an Armenian soldier who is said to have saved him from being killed or captured by the Tsarist forces. However, some Armenians fled from Turkey into Russia, and joined volunteer regiments which the Tsarist authorities were encouraging. In Cilicia, Armenian leaders instigated a revolt against the Ottoman government, but this came to nothing.

Soon events took a tragic turn. Turkish Armenians in the Ottoman army were disarmed and herded into labour battalions, where they were starved, beaten or machine-gunned. On 24 April 1915, 254 Armenian intellectuals in Istanbul were arrested and deported to the provinces of Ayash and Chankiri, where nearly all of them were murdered by the authorities. Further arrests in Istanbul brought the number to 5000.

Having lost both its able-bodied male population (from the army) and now its intellectual elite, the Armenian community was now almost leaderless, and the authorities turned upon it with fury. In every town and village of Turkish Armenia and Asia Minor, the entire Armenian population was ordered out. The men were usually led away and shot down just outside their villages. A far worse fate awaited the women and children: they were forced to walk southwards in huge convoys to the burning deserts of northern Syria. Few survived the privations of these terrible death marches; for months afterwards, the roads and tracks of Anatolia were littered with corpses and skeletons picked clean by the vultures. There were variations on this pattern. In Trebizond, the local Armenians were embarked in boats, and thrown overboard when well out into the Black Sea. A number were despatched by being hurled down the Kemakh Gorge, near Erzinjan.

Those who survived the long journey south were herded into huge open-air concentration camps, the grimmest of which was that at Deir ez-Zor, in Ottoman Syria, where they were starved and killed by sadistic guards. A small number were able to escape through the secret protection of friendly Arabs in villages in northern Syria. Otherwise, the only refugee routes were to Russian Transcaucasia or the Balkans, apart from the remarkable escape of 4000 besieged villagers from Musa Dagh, near Antioch, rescued by a French warship.

Recent scholarship based on Turkish sources has demonstrated beyond doubt the deliberate and official nature of the Armenian genocide.[2] This systematic and successfully executed genocide resulted from decisions taken at the highest government level. The Interior Minister, Talaat Pasha, boasted to Morgenthau, the American ambassador, that the Armenian question was dead for 50 years. The government itself was but an instrument of the Young Turk party, the 'Committee of Union and Progress', whose dominant ideology was pan-Turkism. The mass-murder was not just a matter of 'isolated incidents': it was carefully thought out and executed with precision. Nor did it result from religious intolerance, though the Young Turks mobilized the extremism of the village mullahs, and the greed of poor and deprived Turks. There were in fact Muslim leaders who were shocked by the measures taken, and protested against them.

In recent years the government of the Turkish Republic has, through various official and semi-official channels, strenuously denied that the former Young Turk regime undertook a genocide against the Armenians. It has spent vast sums in propaganda and public relations – various firms in the USA have been hired for the purpose – in order to try to demonstrate that no genocide took place in 1915. Pamphlets are published in Ankara aiming to show that the government orders issued in 1915 were humane; that the Armenians staged a treasonable revolt in Van; that only Armenians near the battle zone were deported; and that the events of 1915 would best be characterized as a civil war between various armed bands.

All these claims are fallacious. As far as the orders are concerned, we know, from the testimony (which is in the Public Record Office, Kew) of an Ottoman Muslim officer who was a participant in the Armenian genocide that there were two sets of orders, one open and the other secret. The secret orders were the ones which had to be obeyed, and they detailed the violent measures to be undertaken against Armenians. Thus for the Turkish government to publish books and pamphlets showing that some orders were benevolent is no more than an exercise in naivete.

As regards Van in April 1915: on the evidence of independent eyewitnesses, the Armenians' defiance of the Turkish governor has been shown to have been self-defence, not rebellion. On the matter of the alleged 'civil war', no reputable military historian gives any grounds for support of this view (least of all the standard work on the subject, Allen and Muratoff's *Caucasian Battlefields*). By equating Turkish and Armenian forces at this time, the proponents of this view are attempting to minimize or ignore the vast power of the Ottoman state, and its extensive deployment of the armed gendarmerie and party officials used to kill Armenian civilians at this time. (Although many Turks and Kurds died also, they died as the result of the spread of disease, not as the result of Armenian policies.)

Who did the killing? In some cases it was ordinary gendarmes. The government also recruited a 'Special Organization' (*Teshkilat-i Makhsusiye*), mostly composed of common criminals released from prison in Western Anatolia, on condition that they engage in the slaughter of the Armenians.

How many Armenians died? Viscount Bryce, speaking in the House of Lords on 6 October 1915, put the figure then at 'around 800,000'. The slaughter continued well into 1916, and later still. The Turkish offensive into the Russian Caucasus in the summer of 1918 claimed many thousands of victims. The Turks then used Armenian refugees as targets for bayonet practice. When the Ottoman army captured Baku in the autumn of 1918, 15,000 Armenians were butchered. Scores of thousands of refugees died of famine after the October Revolution of 1917. As late as 1921, a British colonel in Erzerum found the Kemalists mistreating Armenian captives.

Before 1914, around two million Armenians lived in Ottoman Turkey; since World War I this figure has hardly exceeded 100,000. Thus the number of Armenian dead may safely be put at around 1.5 million. Another half-million became refugees, whose descendants, with their tragic memories, can be found in many countries around the world today.

# 4

# INDEPENDENT ARMENIA: 1918-1920

## Armenians in Tsarist Russia

Armenians had in general prospered from the Russian conquest of the Caucasus. A thrifty and industrious Armenian middle-class grew up in the big cities such as Tiflis in Georgia, and Baku in Azerbaijan. Before the Soviet period, Yerevan in Armenia remained a neglected backwater. However, at the close of the 19th Century, the Armenian population of Caucasia was still largely rural (65%) as against urban (35%). Of the urban population, the majority were working-class people.

In 1836, the Tsarist government issued a regulating statute or *polozhenie*, permitting the Armenian Church to retain its lands, and Armenian schools to keep their autonomy. But during the 1880s, the favour shown to the Armenians began to evaporate. Among the reasons for this was the assassination of Tsar Alexander II in 1881, and the consequent dismissal of his liberal Chief Minister, the Armenian Count Loris-Melikov. In 1884, the Russian authorities closed the senior grades of the Armenian schools; in 1897, when Prince Golitsyn was appointed Governor-General of the Caucasus, he closed the schools altogether. This officious functionary also reduced the number of Armenians in the civil service.

Then Golitsyn struck at the focal point of the Armenian nation: the Apostolic (Gregorian) Church. By a decree of June 1903, the Tsarist authorities nationalized all Armenian Church property. When the clergy resisted, the Russian police occupied Echmiadzin, the seat of the Catholicos, the head of the Armenian Church. The Armenian revolutionaries were now supported by the hitherto hostile bourgeoisie. Cossack terror led to Armenian bombings and shootings.

During the 1905 Revolution, the governor of Baku encouraged the local Tatars in a four-day slaughter of Armenians. The situation was astonishingly similar to that which prevailed in the city in January 1990. Similar excesses took place in several regions of Transcaucasia. In September 1905, mob violence led to serious fires in the Baku oilfields.

Later on, the Armenians gained the upper hand, and worsted the Tatars. These Armeno-Tatar clashes raised the esteem of the Dashnak revolutionary party in the eyes of the peasantry; the Dashnaks were seen to be the only effective armed group prepared to protect the peasants; and the armed power of the party had reversed the anti-Armenian policies of tsarism. However, the vicious clashes left a legacy of hatred between Armenians and Tatars. Right up to the eve of the World War I, Tsar Nicholas II continued to combat Armenian nationalism. In 1911 the Dashnak party was put on trial; defence advocates included Alexander Kerensky and Pavel Miliukov. The trial collapsed in 1912, as Russian policy changed to a pro-Armenian stance for the first time for 30 years.

### Independent Armenia

The recovery of the Armenian nation dates at least symbolically from the declaration of independence of the Armenian Republic on 28 May 1918. The background to this declaration, however, is one of tragedy and remarkable heroism.

After the Bolshevik Revolution of 1917, Russia withdrew from World War I. Lenin and Trotsky signed the Treaty of Brest-Litovsk, which effectively left the Caucasian peoples defenseless before the Turks and their German allies. The Armenians began by forming a federation with the Georgians and the Azerbaijanis (Tatars, Azeris), but the three nationalities found it impossible to agree on a common programme. The Georgians even made a secret pact with the Turks, handing over to them the strategic fortress of Kars. Led by such heroic generals and partisan commanders as Nazarbekov, Dro and Silikov, the Armenians repulsed the Turks at Sardarabad on 22-24 May 1918. The Turks then by-passed the Yerevan district, and captured Baku a few weeks before the Ottoman Empire surrendered to the Allies at the Armistice of Mudros, 30 October 1918.

Thanks to some initial British support, the territory of independent Armenia grew to a size considerably larger than the later Armenian Soviet Socialist Republic, since it came to include Kars and Ardahan, areas which today are in eastern Turkey. But economic conditions were catastrophic. The scenes of famine and privation in the winter of 1918-19 were as bad as the horrors of 1915. Half-a-million refugees, dressed in rags or sacking, roamed the land, or shivered in caves and dugouts. The British Chief Commissioner in Tbilisi, Sir Harry Luke, gives in his autobiography, *Cities and Men*, a vivid account of his three visits to Armenia during that critical period. At the same time, the government of independent Armenia embarked on constructing a republic from a war-torn patch of soil, and by early 1920 its diligence was showing some success. Armenia in the spring of that year was unrecognizable from its condition at the time of independence less than two years before, according to Armenian Prime Minister Simon Vratsian.

For over two years, the Armenians hung on to their independence – literally, 'like grim death'. They had some justification for their 'great expectations'. On 20 December 1917, British Prime Minister Lloyd George had made a speech in Parliament, describing Armenia as 'a land soaked in the blood of innocents', and declaring that it would never be restored to the 'blasting tyranny' of the Turk. In summer 1918, Lloyd George again declared that Britain would not forget its responsibilities to the Armenians; French leaders made similar promises. The American President Woodrow Wilson had a deep personal sympathy for the Armenian cause. In the Twelfth of his Fourteen Points which formed his plan for a post-war settlement, he stated that: 'the other nationalities which are now under Turkish rule should be assured an undoubted security of life and an absolutely unmolested opportunity of autonomous development'.

Relying on these promises, the Armenian leaders came to the Paris Peace Conference with plans for an Armenia stretching from the Black Sea to the Mediterranean. These dreams were later considerably modified, and given international legal recognition in President Wilson's delineation of the Armeno-Turkish frontier (22 November 1920). The over 100,000 sq. km. (40,000 sq. miles) that the American President awarded Armenia constituted, with the exception of the coastline province of Trebizond, areas which had had a substantial Armenian population prior to the genocide, and in some places an overall majority. Wilson's designated territory for Armenia was, however, never implemented since none of the Great Powers was prepared to guarantee it by force of arms, and also there were scarcely 100,000 Armenians still living in the Turkish part of the region, although there were the half-a-million refugees waiting for the ousting of Turkish authority.

During 1919 and 1920, the world situation changed so dramatically that the Allied powers did their utmost to forget their promises to recognize an Armenian state. The British, war-weary and over-extended, evacuated Caucasia, and the Soviets liquidated the White Russian army of General Wrangel in the Crimea. President Wilson, broken in health, faced a hostile Congress, bent on isolationism. Against all the odds, the Turks under Mustafa Kemal, known to the world as Ataturk, staged national recovery, culminating in 1922 with the reoccupation of Smyrna (Izmir), and the liquidation of the British-backed Greek intervention. The Turkish nationalists quickly reached an understanding with Lenin in the Kremlin. In September 1920, the Turkish warlord Kiazim Karabekir Pasha crossed the old 1914 Russo-Turkish frontier, and overran the Kars district. The Bolsheviks closed in from Azerbaijan, and proclaimed a Soviet republic in Yerevan (29 November-2 December 1920). After discussions deep into the night of 30 November, the Dashnak government decided to hand over peacefully to the Bolsheviks; Soviet power appeared to offer more hope to Armenian aspirations than a resistance against greatly superior forces.

The cession of Kars and Ardahan to Turkey was finally confirmed by the Treaty of Kars (13 October 1921). Armenians were not consulted over this treaty which defined their western border. Curiously enough, the treaty also stipulated that the Nakhichevan district, once an integral part of medieval Armenia but later extensively peopled by Tatar Azeris, should be attached to the Soviet Republic of Azerbaijan, based on Baku. The Nakhichevan ASSR is entirely cut off from Soviet Azerbaijan by Armenian territory, and today, 70 years later, forms a resented enclave situated between Soviet Armenia, Iran and Turkey. Similarly Karabagh, an Armenian region where there is still a large Armenian majority, was cut off from Armenia, and left as an enclave within Soviet Azerbaijan.

# 5

## REPUBLICAN TURKEY –
## THE AMBIGUOUS INHERITOR

### The reconstruction period

In the years in which Kemalist Turkey was fighting to establish itself, and to receive international recognition (1919-22), the embryo state showed as much fanaticism and ferocity towards Armenians and Greeks as any of the earlier Turkish states. A few examples suffice to illustrate this ferocity: the Kemalist capture of Marash (February 1920) and of Hadjin (October 1920); the capture of Kars and Alexandropol by the troops of Kiazim Karabekir (October 1920), with its sequel of massacre; and the sack of Smyrna in September 1922[3] and the deliberate destruction by fire of the Armenian quarter, with extensive loss of life. During this last incident naval units of the Western powers stood by offshore, but made virtually no effort to intervene or to put a stop to the atrocities.

However, during the years of the internal reconstruction of Turkey, the Armenians and other Christian minorities were relatively unmolested, except for an outbreak in 1929. There were few Armenians left, and Mustafa Kemal (Ataturk) rightly gauged that the outside powers had lost interest in them. Kemal's attention was fixed on his goal of modernization, and this, coupled with his own personal dislike of religious or social fanaticism for its own sake, meant that on occasion he looked favourably upon Armenians: thus, when Armenians from Kayseri petitioned him in 1928 in the reformed (Latinized) script to permit the re-opening of their church, he immediately assented.

Nevertheless, since the establishment of the Republic of Turkey, the rights of its Armenian citizens have not been fully respected. The main instrument which laid down the principles of the protection of non-Muslim minorities within Turkey was the Treaty of Lausanne (24 July 1923), specifically Articles 38-44. The signatories of this treaty, which terminated the war in the Near East which had been continuing virtually since 1914, were the British Empire, France, Italy, Japan, Greece, Romania and the Serbo-Croat-Slovene state, and Turkey.

Article 38 guaranteed the life and liberty of minorities within Turkey, without distinction of 'birth, nationality, language, race or religion'. It also guaranteed their freedom of movement and of emigration. Article 40 laid down the right of Turkish nationals of non-Muslim minorities 'to establish, manage and control at their own expense any charitable, religious and social institutions, and any schools and other establishments for instruction and education...'. In Article 41 the Turkish government undertook to grant facilities for the minorities to teach their children in their own languages (although they would make the teaching of Turkish obligatory). Article 42 underwrote the legality of the minorities' own customs for regulating their own internal affairs; and the following article upheld the right of the minorities not to be compelled to do anything which their religion forbade. Article 44 gave the foregoing articles international significance, since the League of Nations itself guaranteed them.

These provisions have been, and currently are being, ignored. Due to the achievements of the Kemalists during the 1930s, the great-power rivalry for Turkish support during World War II, and the importance to Nato of Turkish military strength, none of the signatories of the Lausanne settlement has shown the power or the inclination to invoke the Lausanne Treaty, insofar as minority rights are concerned. Yet the provisions remain valid in international law, since the United Nations has been proved to be the legitimate successor organization to the League of Nations in the case of Namibia (South West Africa). At the time the semi-official newspaper *Ileri* commented: 'The Greeks and the Armenians must forget their own language and become Turks or get out.' Rather more crudely, *Ikdam* commented: 'The Armenians in Turkey are to enjoy two privileges only, namely to pray to their God and to bury their dead.'

Relying on the Treaty of Lausanne to protect them, a number of Armenians returned from abroad and laid claim to lands and property from which they and their families had been ousted from 1915 onwards. In country districts, some of these people were hanged by irate Turkish mobs from their own fruit trees, with the encouragement of local gendarmes. Only in Istanbul and a few other cities was it possible for Armenians to resume their interrupted community life. Most areas of the former six 'Armenian *vilayets*' of Eastern Turkey were declared a forbidden military zone. Armenian tourists from abroad, before being granted a visa, were obliged to sign an undertaking not to proceed with legal claims for return of their sequestrated property in Turkey.

Armenian community interests suffered in 1939, when the French mandate over the *sanjak* (district) of Alexandretta – part of Syria – was abandoned in favour of Turkey, in an attempt to propitiate the Turks on the outbreak of World War II. A number of Armenians lived in villages there – the very reduced descendants of outlying districts of medieval Cilician Armenia;[4] and 15,000 of these were unable to contemplate Turkish sovereignty, and left in July 1939 to swell the number of Armenians in Syria and Lebanon to about 200,000.

During World War II, as a manifestation of a revival of pan-Turkism, the government of Ismet Inonu imposed burdensome and discriminatory taxes (*varlik vergisi*) on non-Muslim minorities, especially the Armenian community. Those unable or unwilling to pay were sent, regardless of age, to Eastern Turkey, and made to do forced labour in quarries and on roads, living in atrocious concentration-camp-like conditions. The pro-Nazi sympathies of the Turkish regime and public found expression in March 1943 in the ceremonial repatriation of the mortal remains of Talaat Pasha, who had been assassinated in Germany by an Armenian patriot shortly after World War I. (The assassin was exonerated by a German court, partly on the strength of evidence of Turkish atrocities given by General Liman von Sanders.) A leading Turkish journalist commented that the Turkish nation would be grateful to its government for bringing home Talaat Pasha's remains to his own country – where 'his own ideals had now been realized'. Talaat's reinterment on the Hill of Liberty was attended by representatives of Hitler's ambassador to Turkey, Herr von Papen.

Also during World War II there was an interesting and significant echo of the Armenian genocide. On 22 August 1939 Hitler said to his commanders, 'I have sent to the east my 'Death's Head Units', with the order to kill without pity or mercy all men, women and children of the Polish race. Who still talks nowadays of the extermination of the Armenians?' The remark manifestly connects the genocidal mentality of Hitler with that of the Young Turk leaders – although it did not, at this stage, link the fate planned for the Jews with that of the Armenians, dealing as it did with Poland. It nevertheless shows that an unpunished genocide undertaken by one set of dictators is likely to breed genocidal views in another dictator, leading by an apparently natural progression to a holocaust such as that suffered by European Jewry.

## The post-war period

Since World War II it has been possible for most Armenians in Istanbul to make a living, and indeed live quite comfortably, provided that they abstain from political activity. There has been only one serious out-break of fanaticism, in September 1955 when, after reports of damage to Ataturk's birthplace in Thessaloniki, mobs ran riot in Istanbul, loot-ing and pillaging the shops and property of the minorities. From the mid-1970s largely as a result of the campaign of Armenian terrorism against Turkish diplomats abroad and Turkish airline offices, the posi-tion of Armenians within Turkey has become considerably more pre-carious.

In the official Turkish census report of 1960, the national total of those who speak Armenian as their mother tongue is given as 52,756. The largest concentration was in the Istanbul area, the figure being 37,280. Then came the province of Mardin, with 10,232. The Kasta-monu region contained 1204 Armenian speakers, the Sivas area 565. No other Turkish province numbered more than 500 Armenians – the total for the once flourishing Armenian community of Adana in Cilicia being only six. The district of Van, the ancient heartland of Turkish Armenia, numbered only two persons who dared to list their mother tongue as Armenian.

The undisputed head and spokesman of the Armenian community in modern Turkey, as in the Ottoman Empire, is the Patriarch of the Armenian Apostolic Church in Constantinople. From 1960 to 1990, this position was occupied by the outspoken Patriarch Shnork Kalous-tian, who was tireless in his efforts to protect his Armenian flock from victimization by the Turkish civil and military authorities. His Beati-tude's efforts were hampered and misrepresented by the US State Department, whose pro-Turkish policy aided the success of the Turkish invasion of Cyprus in 1974.

About that time, the State Department sent a special envoy to visit the Armenian Patriarch in Istanbul, on the initiative of Armenian interests in the US. Patriarch Shnork handed the US representative a three-page document, summarizing the grievances of the Turkish Armenians. This document was subsequently suppressed on orders from Washington, the then Secretary of State, Dr. Kissinger, denying that any complaints were voiced by the Patriarch during the US envoy's visit to the Armenian community in Istanbul.

In view of its importance, the Istanbul Memorandum of 1974 is reproduced as Document I. Little of substance has changed in the intervening years, although in the late 1980s, the situation as regards Armenian buildings began to improve. Additional information is given in a summary of Patriarch Kaloustian's 1976 review of problems affect-ing the Armenians in Turkey.[5]

'There are 34 Armenian Apostolic churches in Istanbul and six in the provinces. There are 31 clergymen in Turkey: one bishop, two vartabeds (celibate priests) and 28 kahanas (married priests). Four kahanas and three vartabeds attached to the Patriarchate serve in various countries. The Religious Council held 12 meetings; however, new elections were not held because government permission was not received during the year.

The Kalfayan Orphanage was not able to build a new school, because the authorities had turned down the Armenian request for a new school building permit, despite the fact that the old structure was demolished. The same fate also befell St. Stephen's Church in Khaskugh, which was not able to obtain a permit for a new building construction. The Nersesian School, adjacent to the church, was able to rent a building to use for school purposes in a different section of the city. The legal rights of these two institutions are now being defended in court, demanding justice and proper treatment; the community has assumed heavy and unnecessary financial burden in these matters.

The Sourp Purgich [Holy Savior] Hospital was pressured to pay heavy taxes, and in the past 20 years operational expenses have increased tenfold, while the income of the hospital has virtually remained the same. The government has refused the request by the hospital to raise the income on its various properties. In fact, the government subsidy, which was 100,000 Turkish liras some ten years ago, has been reduced to a mere 15,000 liras without any explanation or reason, creating a difficult situation. The government subsidy of 15,000 liras is less than half the cost per single patient per year.

The harassment in the educational field is more overt. Students whose parents have been Islamized for various reasons, and who have reverted to their original religion, Armenian Apostolic, through legal procedures, are denied the right to attend Armenian schools. If an Armenian has attended a non-Armenian school, he cannot change his mind and attend an Armenian school the following year, despite the fact that Armenian schools are recognized by the Education Ministry as accredited institutions. Another restriction imposed stipulates that Armenian schools cannot accept students from other districts. One of the more obvious pressures is the suppression of the word 'Armenian' from identity cards.'

Turkish government spokesmen have always declined to comment on – or to refute – these charges. Hopes for some improvement in Turkish attitudes towards the Armenian minority in subsequent years have very slowly begun to be fulfilled. Until the late 1980s, the annual reports issued by the Patriarchate spoke of continued failure to solve legal difficulties regarding the church schools and other charitable institutions. Following some sensational articles in the Turkish daily newspaper *Gunaydin*, bombs were thrown at the Armenian patriar-chate, cathedral and school in Istanbul. Damage was relatively slight, and no serious casualties were reported. A similar attack later occurred after the bomb incident at a Turkish bank in London in January 1978. On one occasion the patriarch was assaulted by Turkish youths in his own cathedral.

At one time in 1977, foreign tourists with Armenian surnames were refused entry into Turkey and turned back at the border. This measure was soon rescinded, as was a Ministry of the Interior order closing the Armenian church in the village of Kirk-khan near Iskenderun. To be fair, it must be stated that these events occurred against a background of mounting unemployment and political instability within Turkey, with the growth of the terrorist movement against Turkish diplomats abroad, for which Armenian groups claimed responsibility. (See section on ARMENIAN TERRORISM.)

In the early 1980s, under the military regime in Turkey, there was a revival of pan-Turkish consciousness and nationalist sentiment. This led to a flood of bullying, anti-minority invective in the press, especial-ly directed against the Christian communities, and especially against the Armenians. With tacit government support, the Turkish press insulted and threatened Armenians on an almost daily basis; 'The Armenians should pack up and get out of Turkey', was one of the milder expressions of this mood. Writers demanded vengeance in response to Armenian terrorism abroad.

This racist campaign had a serious effect on the few isolated Turkish Armenians left outside Istanbul. Local Turkish right-wing opinion compelled several of the community to leave Diyarbekir, and the last Armenian had to leave Viranshehir in 1981. Within Istanbul the com-munity was further cowed with fear. Several instances have been reported of the police refusing to come to the assistance of minorities threatened with violence or suffering a physical attack. Despite official claims that Armenians are Turkish citizens like everyone else, it appears that in some areas the rule of law is not extended to them, and that within Turkey itself there are forces pulling Republican Istanbul in the direction of Ottoman Constantinople.

Many foreign scholars and travellers have protested about the neglect and destruction of Armenian cultural monuments in Turkey, such as the blowing-up of the *vank* (monastic complex) of Khtsgonk, which dates from the 6th Century AD and is situated a few miles south of Ani, close to the Soviet-Turkish border. The damage is of such a kind that it cannot have been the result of an earthquake and must have been done by explosives. To deter protest the French archaeologist Dr. Thierry, an expert on medieval Armenian architecture, was arrested by gendarmes in Moush in 1974, and held for three days in a dungeon, without food or water.

In the eastern provinces, those Armenian churches which survive do so through having been converted into barns or local museums. One celebrated church is shown to tourists as an outstanding production by 'early Christian Turks'. The idea of placing these buildings under UNESCO protection has never come to fruition. This is largely due to fear that this step would prove to be their death-warrant – in the same way that property developers in Britain have been known immediately to demolish historic buildings when they are threatened with a preservation order.

Restrictions on Armenians in Turkey continue. In December 1986 Bishop Mesrob Moutafian was arraigned at the Third Criminal Court of Istanbul, along with Sarkis Oflaz, a church lay official, on charges of acting against the law for the protection of historical monuments. Specifically they were accused of temporarily covering a small balcony of the Armenian Patriarchate with material to keep out rain. The prosecutor has asked for five years imprisonment for both men.

Similarly the Turkish state continues to deny an Armenian historical presence. The publisher of a Turkish version of the *Encyclopedia Britannica* was facing prosecution in December 1986 because it contained an article on the existence of an Armenian State in southern Anatolia in the 11th Century.

In 1990 a new Patriarch of Constantinople was elected, following the death of Shnork Kaloustian. Armenian hopes are that Patriarch Karekin Kazandjian will continue to protect his people and their heritage in Turkey.

## Armenian terrorism

Since 1975 some small Armenian groups have engaged in terrorism. This has usually consisted in the assassination of Turkish diplomats, or attacks on Turkish airline and other property, often resulting in indiscriminate killing. Some attacks have taken place in Turkey itself. The impetus for this campaign undoubtedly came from the assassination in Santa Barbara, California, of a Turkish diplomat in January 1973 by Gourgen Yanikian, a 77-year old survivor of the massacres of 1915. This was the first recorded Armeno-Turkish terrorism since 1922. Yanikian's was not the act of a madman, but of a man who had considered matters deeply (if misguidedly) for decades and believed that his course of action was the only one to resolve a sense of desperation.

A couple of years after Yanikian's action, two Armenian groups emerged dedicated to armed action. The first recorded incident was by a group which called itself the Armenian Secret Army for the Liberation of Armenia (ASALA). Its origins can be traced to 1965, to the disaffection of young Armenians with the three existing Armenian political parties of the diaspora and the movement gathered support with the general radicalization that occurred with the Lebanese civil war. Terrorist – or 'revolutionary' – attacks followed, reaching a peak in late 1979, when there were 15 attacks in four months. Only in 1980 were any ASALA members arrested; until then, doubts were expressed that the actions were perpetrated by Armenians. The Turkish government, keen to keep the spotlight away from Armenians, preferred to ascribe the actions to Greek Cypriots.

ASALA's political platform was radical, rhetorical and third-world leftist. It was, however, unquestionably Armenian, and to describe the movement as merely a facet of 'international terrorism' is to ignore ASALA's essential dynamic, and to yield to the fallacious presentation of 'international terrorism' as an indivisible concept, while ignoring the local conditions and historical grievances which create terrorist movements. While there is no doubt that ASALA received help and advice from other groups, its own *raison d'etre* was always Armenian.

Another group, the Justice Commandoes of the Armenian Genocide (JCAG), also claimed responsibility for attacks from 1975. Its programme was largely devoid of leftist rhetoric, concentrating on recognition of the Armenian genocide, and unspecific demands for the return of Armenian lands. In its language and communiques it took a line very close to that of the Dashnak party, leading some to conclude that it was a section of the party. Actions by this group also reached a peak in 1980 but then appeared to disapppear from the scene. Another group, calling itself the Armenian Revolutionary Army, appeared to have taken its place. Other shadowy groups, with names such as the New Armenian Resistance, also surfaced in those years.

The main purpose of Armenian terrorism would appear to be to make Turkey, and the Western world in general, take note of Armenians, and end the guilty and embarrassed silence about them. Terrorism has usually been an instrument of publicity, with any demands in practice merely a way of articulating the group's existence to the world's media. The actions of ASALA and the JCAG should be seen primarily as dramatizing the Armenian genocide – as forcing the issue to the attention of Turkey, and its allies and sponsors in Europe and America. The Armenian experience of 1915 has been written out of the script of 20th Century political consciousness since the 1923 Treaty of Lausanne. The terrorist groups were by their violent methods determined to make the issue a current one again, claiming (wrongly) that peaceful methods had failed.

Armenian terrorism has abated from the mid-1980s. This appears to be partly because of splits within ASALA, after a particularly grisly and random series of episodes in France in November 1983, which followed the arrest of an Armenian at Orly airport. In addition, the Israeli invasion of Lebanon in June 1982 destroyed a substantial part of ASALA's training facilities and infrastructure. It is possible, too, that the airing of the Armenian question at the United Nations Sub-Commission on the Prevention of Discrimination and Protection of Minorities in Geneva in August 1985 has deflated the claims of the proponents of terror, who insist that Armenians have met only with silence for 70 years, and that terror is legitimized by the refusal of any other party to listen.

By any standards, even the most corrupt, there is in fact no justification for Armenian terrorism, since the articulation of Armenian claims is still in its infancy. Armenians have been surprisingly backward at expressing political hopes sensibly and rationally in modern political language, and in supporting their demands with accurate facts and figures, and clear and unambiguous historical details. Despite the amount of outrage expressed over the Armenian genocide, it loses much of its political meaning given the absence of well-presented, coherent research telling the interested but uninformed public about what happened and why it happened, backed up with names, dates and places. The terrorist response is – to put it mildly – premature, when so little straightforward research and historical writing has been carried out – other than the statutory repetition of 'what great Western figures have said about the Armenians', which many Armenians mistake for the story of their people in their original towns and villages. A few organizations, such as the Zoryan Institute of Cambridge, Massachusetts, have begun to work on collecting and publishing relevant genocide material, but their findings have not filtered down yet to the consciousness of the majority. Armenian terrorism appears to have died out completely following the emergence of the struggle for Karabagh.

Turkey has said it is opening its archives on the Armenian genocide; but in fact many things about the nature and planning and execution of the events of 1915 can be discovered by using printed sources.[6] Vital questions regarding the Ottoman archives are : how complete are the archives which the Turkish government is opening?; and, where are the archives of the Party, the Committee of Union and Progress, which instigated the Armenian genocide and which was more powerful than the fabric of the Ottoman state itself.

## DOCUMENT I

### RESTRICTIONS ON THE ARMENIAN COMMUNITY IN TURKEY (1974)

#### I. Real estate and financial restrictions

1. Many Armenian church people would like to donate their properties to the Armenian churches, hospitals and orphanages, as endowments. The authorities concerned however do not recognize such endowments, and sometimes they confiscate them, as has happened in at least one case, namely that of the Armenian hospital in Yedikuleh.
2. The authorities concerned refuse to hand over the ownership papers for those church properties, for which a law court decision has already been made in favour of the communal religious or charitable organizations.
3. The authorities concerned consistently refuse to give permission to build new buildings on vacant church properties, from which, however, they continue to assess property taxes.
4. Permission for repair and restoration, sometimes even proper maintenance, of churches, schools, orphanages etc. is given only after immense difficulties, and long delays.
5. Two churches and two orphanages, one for boys, called Nersesian, and the other for girls, called Kalfayan, have been demolished in the section of Halicioglu of Istanbul, due to the construction of another bridge over the Golden Horn. The civil authorities have not as yet given permission to replace the demolished buildings with new ones. The orphanages continue to exist in rented buildings, which is a great financial burden. This has resulted in greatly reduced services to the poor children of the community.
6. The sale price of the demolished buildings and other properties seized by the Bridge Construction Authorities has not been given to

these communal organizations, but put in trust, pending presentation of the title deeds of properties.

7. A regulation promulgated in 1936, says that apart from normal operational expenses, the communal authorities cannot spend more than 250 liras without the permission of **Vakiflar** [religious property trust] authorities. This regulation was not enforced until recently but is now strictly observed. Those in authority ignore the fact that the value of 250 liras in 1936 was equivalent to approximately 20-25,000 Turkish liras in 1974.

8. The **Vakiflar** authorities have recently levied 5% surtax upon the income of communal organizations, which have already paid their government and municipal taxes. This surtax is levied also upon the special collections made to balance the budget of the organization.

9. Upon selling a communal property, the **Vakiflar** authorities demand that the money from the sale of any property be deposited in the **Vakiflar Banks**. The capital is frozen, and the communal organizations can never withdraw it, although they receive a nominal interest on the capital.

## II. Educational Restrictions

1. There are very strict controls upon the Armenian communal schools – 32 in number. Despite the fact that the Armenian directors of the schools are Turkish citizens, the Educational Department has also appointed a Turkish 'sub-director', who is the 'de facto' director of the school, and without the approval of the latter, the 'de jure' Armenian director cannot act. The aim is to 'Turkify' the Armenian schools as much as possible.

2. The directors of Armenian schools, although appointed by the communal authorities, must be approved in addition by the Educational Department. Recently in the majority of cases and after long delay, the Education Department has refused to confirm them. Usually they refuse to confirm directors who are strong and capable and approve mediocre ones. During the last three years at least four appointed directors were refused confirmation by the Education Department and at present there are at least three schools without Armenian directors, which are managed by Turkish 'sub-directors'.

3. The Armenian school authorities are having great trouble in finding teachers for their primary schools. Until recently any graduate from an Armenian Lycee – senior High School – could teach in any Armenian Primary School. Now they cannot, as an order of the Education Department requires a Teacher's Certificate from every Primary School

45

Teacher. The Armenians would not object to this regulation, if facilities were given for the candidates to promote their Armenian language studies. There are no such facilities. The Armenian teacher candidate, after finishing eight years of education in his or her communal school, can enrol in the government Teachers College, and graduate from it in four years. By the time he – or she – has graduated, he has usually forgotten most of the Armenian language he has been taught. Teachers are supposed to teach in the Armenian language in the communal Primary Schools. The Armenian schools now need at least 25 additional Armenian teachers for their own Primary Schools. Since these are not available, the vacancies are now filled by Turkish teachers.

4. Recently the most capable directress of an Armenian Lycee was removed from her office without any stated reason.

5. Any so-called 'Mufettish' or inspector, can go to any Armenian school at any time and ask questions, many on trivial matters. They have been known to ask, for example, why the schools receive correspondence in Armenian, or in any other foreign language . . . Why the students say prayers at the dinner table in the refectories? (Students are not allowed to pray in the classrooms at any time.)

6. In 1973 'Mufettishes' expelled from an orphanage-school 10 small boys giving as the reason that 'they don't know the Armenian language'.

7. Just at the beginning of 1973-1974 academic year, an order came from the Education Department to the effect that all the new students, and those who were changing their schools, must not register at school until they have obtained a permit from the Education Department. This caused unnecessary delays. There are cases where some of the children got their permission only three months after the opening of schools. About 40-50 students did not get permission for the simple reason that the religion of their fathers or grandfathers was written in the state record offices, as 'Christian' (without the addition of the word 'Armenian') or 'Armenian Orthodox', which the authorities consider a denomination other than the Armenian Apostolic Church (which is definitely not the case). These bureaucratic reasons for refusals reveal the real intention of the authorities concerned, namely to reduce the numbers of Armenian students.

8. The authorities have refused to give permission to transform at least some schools into boarding schools for poor children, particularly those coming from the needy families of Asia Minor, who need better care, better shelter, and better nourishment, than they have at home. The communal organizations are now caring for these poor children in ordinary rented houses, which besides creating accommodation diffi-

culties, is an extra financial burden.

These are some of the restrictions which are openly contrary not only to the provisions of the Treaty of Lausanne, but also to the Constitution of the country, because parents are free to send their children to any school they prefer. Secondly, there is no law against transforming any private school – *ozel okul* – into a boarding school as long as legal requirements have been fulfilled. These restrictions, besides being against the law, in most cases are also against elementary human rights and conscience.

## III. General Restrictions

Other restrictions, which are neither financial nor educational, include the following:

1. From ancient times through the Republican period and up to the downfall of the Menderes regime, the Armenian Community had a Central Executive Committee. In 1960 it was abolished. It is a fundamental law in the Armenian Church, that all communities, besides having their local Executive Committee, must also have their Central Executive Committee or Council. This is the situation in the USA, in France, in the Middle East, and even in Soviet Armenia. Only in Turkey is the Armenian Community deprived of its own Central Council at present.

2. The authorities permitted the Religious Council of the Armenian Church in Turkey to continue its existence and function. The last Religious Council was elected in 1961, with the election of the present Patriarch. The Council is composed of nine members, four of whom have since died. The Patriarch has applied to the authorities to give permission to elect a new Council according to the rules and regulations of the Church. No permission has ever been received.

3. The formal common names of all the communal organizations has always been 'Mufetelli Heyeti'. In 1965, the 'Vakiflar' Department changed it into 'Yonetim Kurulu'; when asked why this change was made, the answer was that they were changing the old Arabic expression into modern Turkish. However, it was later found that the terms had very important different legal definitions. The first one meant a *vakif* organization with all rights of property ownership – selling, buying, building, repairing, restoring, etc., whereas the second one was only a managing body without any ownership rights. Thus the authorities argue that the communal organization can no longer purchase or possess new properties nor receive such properties, even as a gift or in a will. The authorities concerned also refuse to hand over title deeds to

the communal organizations for properties, for which they had not obtained the title deeds earlier for one reason or another.

# 6

## ARMENIANS IN THE DIASPORA

Deportations and mass emigration from the homeland have been a tragic feature of Armenian history for centuries. The dispersion began in the early medieval period, was intensified during Sultan Abdul Hamid's massacres of 1895-96, and reached a climax during the Young Turk genocide of 1915. The only consolation is that the condition of exile has served to develop the resourcefulness of the Armenian character, and provide a world-wide outlet for Armenian dynamism and professional acumen. Such qualities have reached their highest point outside Soviet Armenia in the USA, but it is encouraging to report that Armenians in most countries constitute a prosperous, well integrated group.

### The Americas

By far the most prosperous and internationally important diaspora community is that of the USA and Canada. Large groups of Armenians live in Fresno in California and at Watertown, a suburb of Boston, Massachusetts; however, the highest concentration of US Armenians is today around Los Angeles. The Armenian population of the USA and Canada, calculated two decades ago as around 450,000 strong, is now possibly one million and increasing rapidly. In California their growth has been especially strong over the past decade; from 81,000 in 1980 to over 400,000 in 1990.[7] The most recent migrants are from Soviet Armenia.

Until recently the most visible Armenian public figure was George Deukmejian, Governor of California from 1982 to 1990. Currently, there is no Armenian state governor or congressman. One of the most visible Armenian public figures is Vartan Gregorian, President of Brown University, Rhode Island. Born in Tabriz, Iran, he was president of the New York Public Library before taking up his academic post. Of those Armenians who take part in business and charitable activities, of particular note is Alex Manoogian, whose success as a businessman has been matched by his unstinting generosity to Armenian (and non-

Armenian) causes. Other Armenians in the public eye are Kerk Kerkorian, the Los Angeles financier; and, in Canada, the distinguished photographer Yousuf Karsh, who was born in Mardin, Turkey. In the American context, mention should also be made of the painter Arshile Gorky (born in Van with the name Vosdanik Adoian), who died in 1949, who was the founder of the movement known as Abstract Expressionism. Some of his early paintings are imbued with a deep responsiveness to village life and traditions in Armenia, as well as to the spectacular scenery of the homeland. The writer, William Saroyan, who died in 1981, was of Armenian descent.

Armenians in the US tend to be highly educated. One survey found that 57% were in professional or managerial posts and that 45% had completed university. They also support an Armenian school system with 11 private elementary schools in Los Angeles alone, and others elsewhere in the US and Canada. In addition, they have established a state-approved American-Armenian International College at La Verne, in Los Angeles, and two Chairs in Armenian Studies at the University of California in Los Angeles.[8] and there is also a Chair at Columbia University, New York.

There are many Armenian organizations based in the USA. Among them are the energetic Hairenik Association of Boston (Dashnak, activist and publishers of the *Armenian Weekly*, and the daily *Hairenik*), the Baikar Association of Boston (Armenian Democratic Liberal Organization, Ramgavar, publishers of the weekly *Mirror-Spectator* and *Baikar*), the popular and more conservative Armenian General Benevolent Union (AGBU), founded in 1906 in Cairo, Egypt.

The AGBU itself was reorganized during the 1915 genocide to set up refugee camps, rescue orphan children from the desert, and generally salvage the remnants of the shattered Armenian people dispersed throughout the Near East. Today the AGBU supports Armenian schools, charities and other good causes throughout the world. There are several AGBU schools in Lebanon, Latin America, the United States, and the Melkonian Institute in Nicosia, Cyprus. (Another major international agency with Armenian origins is the Calouste Gulbenkian Foundation in Lisbon). There is also the Armenian Relief Society, affiliated with the Dashnak community, founded in 1910 in New York to undertake world-wide Armenian relief. During the period of the republic it was recognized by the ICRC as the 'Armenian Red Cross'. Today, the ARS is active world-wide in assisting the welfare of the Armenian people.

The growth of the political clout of the Armenian lobby has been remarkable since 1976. Notable has been its sponsorship of a House

Joint Resolution in Congress, seeking to declare 24 April a national day of remembrance for 'man's inhumanity to man'. Every April there are meetings, demonstrations and picketings of Turkish consular buildings, showing that, however close is the strategic relationship between the US and Turkey, Armenians are determined to have the right to their own history.

Armenian journalism in the United States is represented by five Armenian English-language newspapers, including the *Armenian Weekly* (Boston), the *Armenian Reporter* (New York), the *Armenian Mirror-Spectator* (Watertown), the *Armenian Observer* (Los Angeles), and the *California Courier* (Los Angeles). Major Armenian language newspapers are *Baikar* (Watertown), *Hairenik* (Boston), *Asbarez* (Los Angeles), as well as *Nor Or* (Los Angeles).

There are also substantial Armenian communities in the main cities of **Canada**, with a recent shift of population from the traditional centre of Montreal to Toronto. The total number of Armenians in Canada may be in the region of 60,000. In South America the largest community – 80,000 to 100,000 strong – is in **Argentina**, supporting a bilingual daily paper. Judge Leon Arslanian was presiding judge in the 1985-86 trial in Buenos Aires of General Galtieri and the other leaders of the former Argentine junta and is internationally recognized as a firm upholder of human rights in Latin America. There are smaller Armenian communities in **Uruguay**, **Venezuela** and **Brazil**.

The church life of Armenians in America is active. There are over 90 parishes, most of which have cultural and recreational facilities, located around the major cities of the east, central states and west coast. A seminary, St. Nerses, opened in 1962, is presently associated with St. Vladimir's Orthodox Seminary in New York.

## Western Europe

The Armenian link with **France** is of considerable antiquity, dating back to the time of the Crusades. The last king of Armenia is buried in St. Denis. Today, the community is the most important in Europe. It numbers about 350,000,[9] and is centred mainly in Paris, Marseille, Lyon and their suburbs. The Armenian Apostolic Church has 16 churches, including the cathedral of St. John the Baptist, Paris and it also runs a school for girls just outside Paris. Armenian Catholics are well established in France, with eight parishes throughout the country. They also run boarding schools outside Paris. There are also a small group of Armenian Protestants who have been very active in relief work in the wake of the Armenian earthquake.

Cultural matters are well cared for among French Armenians. In addition to thriving organizations run by churches or political organizations, there is a fine research library in the capital, the Bibliotheque Nubarian, in Place Alboni. It was founded by the AGBU, and contains over 10,000 volumes in several languages. There are two daily newspapers – *Haratch*, founded in the 1920s and the bilingual *Gamk*, the organ of the Dashnaks. About a dozen Armenian language or joint Armenian-and-French language magazines and journals are published. Armenians are well integrated into the French cultural scene – one has only to think of household names like Charles Aznavour, Sylvie Vartan, Anouk Aimee, Henri Verneuil (born Ashot Malakian), Henri Troyat (born Torossian), a leading French writer, and the painters Carzou and Jansen. French Armenians were in the early 1980s heartened by the support given to their cause by the recognition of the 1915 genocide by President Mitterrand.

The Armenian community in **United Kingdom** (UK), numbering about 15,000, is also well established, especially in London and Manchester. The Manchester community dates back to the 1840s, and played a part in the 19th Century textile boom. The ranks of the London Armenians have been swelled by refugees from disaster areas such as the Lebanon, Cyprus, and most recently, Iran. London has two Apostolic churches, and the Armenian House cultural centre. The Supreme Catholicos at Holy Echmiadzin maintains his personal representative, accredited to the Archbishop of Canterbury. Prominent Armenian musicians include the Chilingirian String Quartet and the conductor Loris Tjeknavorian, who has returned to Armenia to head the Philharmonic Orchestra. The AGBU, the Armenian Relief Society, the Armenian National Committee (a lobbying group), and the Calouste Gulbenkian Foundation of Lisbon, all maintain branches in London. The Centre for Armenian Information and Advice (CAIA), established in 1985, provides a range of services for Armenian refugees, including education, training and advice.

The Armenian colony in **Italy** is of long standing, reflecting the Papacy's traditional friendship with Armenia. The Armenian Catholic order of the Mekhitarists has a monastery on the island of San Lazzaro at Venice. The order was founded over 250 years ago in Constantinople, and later went to San Lazzaro at the invitation of the Venetian Republic. It was dedicated to the dissemination of knowledge, and played a vital role in the Armenian emancipation movement from about 1800. The English poet Byron learnt Armenian here in 1816. The monastery has a valuable library – the second largest collection of Armenian manuscripts in the world – which was damaged by fire in

1975. Unfortunately the monastery was at one stage a victim of unwise speculative investments, and became bankrupt, although this was overcome after assistence from the Armenian diaspora. This in itself is a curious plight for a monastery to find itself in, but what was truly alarming was the prospect that San Lazzaro might have been compelled to sell off all or part of its remarkable historical and artistic treasures. San Lazzaro continues to act as a cultural centre. Substantial Armenian industrial and business interests exist in Milan, which is the centre of the bishopric and the main Armenian community, Rome and Venice.

The Armenian community in **Germany** is less prominent today than in pre-war times but more recent growth gives a total of about 15,000. However, there is an active communal organization, whose president resides in Berlin. Some Armenian carpet merchants in London have subsidiaries in Dusseldorf. The Armenian church fellowship in Cologne operates under the patronage of the German Cardinal-Archbishop there. At the University of Heidelberg there is a German-Armenian cultural society. There is also an Institute of Armenian Affairs in Munich, directed by Edward Hovannessian.

In **Austria**, the Armenian community is centred in Vienna, where the Catholic Mekhitarist Fathers have a magnificent library, and publish a renowned scholarly journal; they also operate a commercial printing works. The importance of the community is recognized by the existence of an Apostolic church, subordinated to Echmiadzin. The **Swiss** Armenians have redoubled their activity in Geneva in recent years. In an attractive city suburb, they have built and consecrated a handsome new Apostolic church.

## Eastern Europe

The East European Armenian diaspora has a long and interesting history, going back to the Byzantine era. In **Poland** and in Hapsburg-dominated Transylvania and Hungary, the Armenians were obliged to adopt Roman Catholicism, which led to a certain loss of identity. However, Armenians have played a distinguished part in the intellectual, commercial and ecclesiastical life of modern Poland, and are well respected there.

Before World War II, some 50,000 Armenians lived in **Romania**. They dominated the entire northern quarter of Suceava, the former capital of Moldavia and owned a fortified monastery (Zamca), dating from about 1600. The trade of Jassy, Moldavia's modern capital, was largely in their hands. Bucharest is the centre of an Armenian Apostolic bishopric, once occupied by the present Supreme Catholicos, Vazken I. The handsome Armenian cathedral in Bucharest was completed in 1915. After World War II, the Communist regime was hostile to private enterprise. Most of the local Armenians emigrated to the Armenian SSR, to America, or to Lebanon. Only about 5000 remained behind. In 1973, however, the general manager of the main Bucharest department store was an Armenian and the Minister of Machine Tool Production in the Romanian government was Mr. Virgile Aktarian. There were also noted Armenian opera singers and actors. An Armenian weekly paper, *Nor Giank* ('New Life'), appeared in Bucharest. Little news of the Armenians has emerged from Romania since the overthrow of communism.

Armenians have done well in **Bulgaria**, where they number about 20,000. Unlike other minorities, only the Armenians and the Jews were recognized during the Zhivkov era, having their own cultural and youth organizations. The main Armenian centres are at Plovdiv, Sofia, Varna and Ruse. They have several clubs, guest houses, theatres and choral societies. The flourishing churches come under the jurisdiction of the Armenian bishop in Romania, the Reverend Dirair Mardikian.

## Near and Middle East

The metropolis of the western Armenian diaspora has for half a century been Beirut, the Lebanese capital, still torn asunder by the effects of civil war which has continued with varying intensity since 1976. The **Lebanon** must now be considered an Armenian disaster area.

The Armenians (perhaps 175,000 in the mid-1980s and 100,000 in 1990) in the early 1980s constituted 7% of the entire Lebanese population, and were the seventh largest community there. The majority live in Beirut and its suburbs. They include wealthy businessmen, farmers, and poor workers and peasants. The Catholicos of the Great House of Cilicia (Antilias), the Patriarch of the Armenian Catholics, and the President of the Union of Armenian Evangelical Churches in the Middle East, all have headquarters in the Beirut area. Before the outbreak of the civil war, 60 Armenian schools – kindergartens, primary schools and high schools – and the Haigazian College and the Nshan Palandjian Academy, were operating in the Lebanon. There are over 20 Armenian churches, four daily newspapers, and more than a dozen weekly, monthly and quarterly magazines. The three major political parties – the Dashnaks (ARF), the more cautious Ramgavars, and the socialist Hunchaks – all play their role in the political, cultural and athletic life of the community. The Dashnaks have the headquarters of their

Homenetmen sporting club in Beirut, a world-wide organization with 17,000 members. The Hunchaks also have their similar but smaller Homenmen organization based there.

Armenians long played an important, though secondary, role in the business world of Beirut. The devastation of that city is a disaster which has repercussions for Armenians all over the world. Throughout almost all the fighting, the Armenians had sought to maintain a neutral stance. However, an estimated 1000 Armenians had been killed by September 1986, and many thousands wounded. According to an Armenian Revolutionary Federation spokesman, damage to Armenian property had reached $US 200 million. Many Armenians have left the country, and those who stayed behind were at one time menaced by famine. The murderous 1989 bombardment and subsequent exodus from Beirut was only the latest chapter in the flight of the Armenian community from the Lebanon often to sanctuary organized by the Armenian diaspora around the world.

Armenians in **Cyprus** suffered during the 1974 Turkish invasion. In Nicosia, the Melkonian High School was hit by a Turkish bomb and its reconstruction has cost the AGBU about $US one million. Armenians in the northern sector of Cyprus have been turned out of their homes and shops, and beaten up. In Famagusta and elsewhere, Armenian churches and monuments have been vandalized or demolished by settlers from the Turkish mainland, Turkish villagers or units of the Turkish armed forces. As with many other Lebanese, Cyprus has provided a new base and the Armenian community has grown steadily.

Serious problems of another kind beset the Armenians of **Iran**, about 120,000 strong. From the 17th Century Armenian township of New Julfa, close to Isfahan, the main Armenian population centre has shifted to Tehran. Here the community has several churches and cultural institutions. Before the Shah's overthrow in 1979, Tehran Armenians owned many prosperous business concerns, including breweries. Current economic and political upheavals have proved serious to Armenian interests here, while religious fundamentalists have attempted to restrict the operation of Tehran's Armenian schools. In June 1984, the Iranian government temporarily closed Armenian schools during the visit of the Turkish Prime Minister. Nevertheless, Armenians are free to commemorate 1915 every April; and there is an Armenian cultural and sporting club. A newspaper, *Alik*, is published. The historic Armenian community in Tabriz, capital of Iranian Azerbaijan, is also of contemporary importance. It has an archbishopric subordinate to the Great House of Cilicia, with an interesting museum. From Tabriz to Tehran, thousands of Armenians still make an annual pilgrimage in July to the

14th Century church of St. Thaddeus, on the south side of Mount Ararat.

Armenians are found in virtually all main cities of the Near East. In **Egypt**, the Armenian connection goes back to the 11th Century Fatimid Grand Vizier Badr al-Jamali, who was an Armenian and served from 1073 to 1074; and in modern times to the officials who served the dynasty of Muhammad Ali, notably Nubar Pasha, who became prime minister. More recently, the Cairo Armenians lost much ground following the withdrawal of British power and the growth of local nationalism, but of those who remain – perhaps 10,000 in all – some are prospering.

In **Syria**, the largest Armenian community is in Aleppo, where they are prominent in hotel management and in medicine. Many Armenians left Beirut for Aleppo and today the Armenian population of the city is between 70,000 and 80,000. There is a much smaller community in Damascus. Until his retirement General Karamanougian was counted prominent in the leadership of the Syrian army. Armenian schools in Syria have had their curricula severely reduced over the years. The community in **Iraq** is also substantial, totalling perhaps 20,000; 70% of Iraqi Armenians live in Baghdad; the rest in Basra or Kirkuk/Mosul. However, the dictatorial nature of the Iraqi regime has allowed the community little freedom. The Armenian church in central Baghdad was damaged as a result of allied bombing in the Gulf War. In 1990 there was also reported to be an Armenian community in **Kuwait**, although its fate after the Iraqi invasion of August 1990 is unclear. There is an active Armenian community in **Jordan**, which a few years ago built itself a church in Amman. Many Jordanian Armenians are 'double refugees', having fled from Palestine during the war of 1948-9, in addition to their flight from their homeland.

In **Israel** there is a small but flourishing community in Jaffa, about 300 in number, although in recent years it has been troubled by factionalism. In Jerusalem, in the section of the city which Israel captured from Jordan during the 1967 war, there is an ancient and venerable community, centering around the cathedral and monastery of St. James. The monastery owns a printing press, which published its journal *Sion*, from 1866 to 1877, and in more recent years; the Gulbenkian Library there is also noteworthy. The present patriarch who took office in 1990, His Beatitude Torkom Manougian, is a distinguished and dedicated man. He was formerly Archbishop of the Eastern Diocese in the United States, based in New York; before that, he was one of the brothers in the Jerusalem monastery. He has approached the complex task of being Patriarch of Jerusalem with great dignity and sense of responsibility. Among his first activities has been the cataloguing and inventorying of all properties belonging to the Patriarchate.

## India and South East Asia

The great days of the Armenian presence in India both preceded and coincided with those of the British Raj – from the early 18th to the mid-20th Century. The Armenians of Bombay and Calcutta played a great role in international trade with Europe, with Persia and the Ottoman Empire, and with the Far East. They were highly cultured, well educated, and strongly patriotic, and financed many useful enterprises. After the 1947 withdrawal of the British, who favoured the Armenians as Christians, the community has languished somewhat, and many Indian Armenians have emigrated.

This applies also to the once-flourishing Armenian colonies in Rangoon and in Singapore. Armenians held important positions at court in 18th Century **Burma**, and more recently those of **Singapore** played a prominent part in setting up the independent state there in 1965, and made their administrative and political talent available at the highest ministerial level. The Armenian-founded Raffles Hotel remains outstanding.

## Africa

Armenians have engaged in trade, diplomacy and missionary work in Africa since the medieval times. The ports of East Africa have attracted their business talent while Armenians have been active in **South African** industrial centres such as Johannesburg and Cape Town. Particularly interesting is the long-established Armenian colony in **Ethiopia**. The Armenian Apostolic Church has close links with the national Church of Ethiopia. The late Bishop Derenik Poladian (murdered in 1963) was for some years Dean of the Ethiopian national Church's seminary in Addis Ababa.

## Australia

Among the younger Armenian communities, that of Australia is one of the most dynamic. There are about 30,000 Armenians in Australia, mainly in Sydney and Melbourne. The Armenian church in Sydney is directed by a bishop, that in Melbourne by a *Vardapet* (doctor of theology). The communities publish two monthly journals and organizes cultural events which are open to the Australian public. Apart from many individuals engaged in commerce and industry, the Australian Armenians include university lecturers, engineers, doctors of medicine, scientific workers and people engaged in music and the fine arts. There is also a radio station broadcasting in Armenian.

# 7

# SOVIET ARMENIA – A NATIONAL HOME

The Armenians, despite their history of persecution, oppression and dispersion continue to display a determination for survival and a high degree of national self-awareness. Perhaps 2.5 million Armenians live in the diaspora and communities throughout the world, but the majority live in the former Armenian Soviet Socialist Republic (SSR), since August 1990 the Republic of Armenia, where they comprise 90% of the 3.3 million population. Another 1.3 million live elsewhere in the USSR, mainly in neighbouring Georgia and, until recently, in Azerbaijan. The earthquake of December 1988, in which 28,000 died, the violence generated by the conflict with Azerbaijan and the re-emergence of Armenian political nationalism have focused world attention on Transcaucasian Armenia.

## The early years

The Soviet Republic of Armenia set up at the end of 1920 began its life in conditions scarcely less grim than those prevailing when independent Armenia was established less than three years previously. The economic situation had improved little since 1917. Heavy snow blocked the roads, isolating Armenia from the outside world. The *Revkom* or Revolutionary Committee resolved to 'requisition and confiscate food from private individuals in the cities, and grain from the peasants'. Parties of soldiers, heavily armed, proceeded to every house, rich or poor, and forcibly removed all rice, wheat and oats, tinned or condensed milk. Sheep and cattle were taken away from the peasants. Personal property, such as carpets, jewellery, even overcoats, were taken as well, and barbers' shop appliances, beehives and musical instruments were 'expropriated' by the Bolsheviks.

These excesses, and the general despair of the starving population, soon provoked an uprising headed by the surviving leaders of the Dashnak party, who attacked Yerevan and deposed the local Soviet regime. But the Armenian Dashnak triumph was short-lived. In neighbouring Georgia, the Red Army conquered the local Menshevik gov-

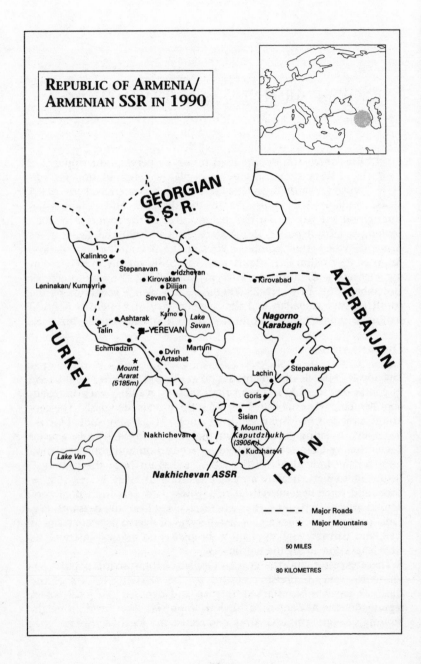

REPUBLIC OF ARMENIA/
ARMENIAN SSR IN 1990

GEORGIAN S. S. R.

Kalinino

Stepanavan

Idzhevan

Leninakan/ Kumayri

Kirovakan

Kirovabad

Dilijan

Sevan

AZERBAIJAN

Ashtarak

Kamo

Lake Sevan

Nagorno Karabagh

Talin

YEREVAN

TURKEY

Echmiadzin

Dvin

Martuni

Artashat

Lachin

Stepanakert

Mount Ararat (5185m)

Goris

Sisian

Mount Kaputdzhukh (3906m)

Nakhichevan

Kudsharavi

IRAN

Lake Van

Nakhichevan ASSR

- - - - Major Roads
★   Major Mountains

50 MILES

80 KILOMETRES

ernment in February 1921. The Soviet forces then turned on Armenia, and Yerevan was retaken from the Dashnaks on 2 April 1921. In the mountainous region of Zangezur, several thousand Dashnaks continued their resistance until, exhausted, they fled across the border into Persia in July.

Soviet Armenia is even smaller than independent Armenia had been, and embodies only a tenth of historical 'Great Armenia'. Kars, Ardahan and Igdir were by 1921 already firmly in Turkish hands. The region of Surmalu, on the northern slopes of Mount Ararat, in which Igdir is situated, became part of Turkey, even though it had never been an integral part of the Ottoman Empire: in 1827 Russia had captured it from Persia. Thus the Turkish republic could claim no historical right to it. This was implicitly acknowledged by Mustafa Kemal, since he never even claimed it in his maximalist 'National Pact'. To wipe out local patriotism in Armenia, Georgia and Azerbaijan, Stalin merged several territories into a single Transcaucasian federation. This arrangement continued until the local leadership had been thoroughly purged by firing squad and Siberian exile. The republics did not emerge as separate entities until after the promulgation of the Stalin constitution in 1936.

The Soviet leadership under Stalin set out to make Transcaucasia, particularly Georgia and Armenia, a show-place. They rebuilt Armenia so that it would be a focus for the Armenian diaspora all over the world. Although the Dashnak leadership of independent Armenia had resisted the Soviet take-over, a number of eminent Armenian revolutionaries had worked in the Leninist tradition – Stepan Shahumian, one of the 26 Baku Commissars murdered by British-backed elements in 1918; Kamo (Ter-Petrossian), whose daring exploits enriched the Bolshevik party funds; the young poet Vahan Terian, who advised Lenin on Turkish Armenia; Alexander Miasnikian, Armenia's prime minister in 1921; A.I. Mikoyan, one of the few Old Bolsheviks to survive the Stalin purges.

Foreign relief organizations, organized by dedicated individuals such as the Reverend Harold Buxton, helped to feed Armenia's teeming refugees. The dreaded *Cheka* (OGPU) at least ensured public security of a kind – in that the Armenian peasant was no longer murdered by Turkish soldiers and Kurdish tribesmen. The Leninist New Economic Policy (NEP) provided a flexible framework within which the small shopkeeper and craftsman could make a modest living – until the clamp-down which attended the Five-Year Plan campaign from 1928 onwards.

Symptomatic of the resurgence of Armenian cultural life in the Soviet orbit was the foundation of Yerevan University in 1921. Two years later, in 1923, the distinguished Armenian architect Alexander Tamanian, Vice-President of the Russian Academy of Fine Arts, was sent from Moscow to Yerevan to plan the rebuilding of Yerevan on modern lines, but with due regard for Armenian national traditions in building and sculpture. He also rebuilt Stepanakert, the new capital of Karabagh.

## Post-war Armenia

In Soviet Armenia today, Armenian (with its distinctive script) is the first language, although of course Russian is an official language. Far more people speak Armenian than Russian. Soviet Armenia is the only region of the world where official business is conducted primarily in the Armenian vernacular. Armenia also has a first-rate public education system. An Armenian branch of the Soviet Academy of Sciences was founded in 1935, and promoted in 1943 to the status of an independent Academy. Associated with the Academy is the Byurakan Observatory (with its immense 2.6 metre telescope), directed by Academician Viktor Hambartsumian, well known in international astronomical circles.

The economic and cultural resurgence of Soviet Armenia provoked dissension among the Armenian diaspora, especially between World War I and World War II. Many old Dashnaks regarded the USSR as an arch-enemy, surpassed in wickedness only by the Turks. Others came to see the fostering of a national home in Soviet Armenia as the only hope for preserving the national ethos in the harsh and competitive circumstances of the 20th Century. Sometimes the division in outlook took tragic forms, as when in 1933 a leading Armenian cleric suspected of pro-Soviet sympathies was murdered during a service in a New York church. Today, however, the situation is radically changed, and the old parties are striving to make themselves relevant in the re-born post-perestroika Republic of Armenia.

Immediately after World War II, Stalin embarked on a forward policy in Transcaucasia, with a view to annexing Persian Azerbaijan, Kurdistan, and parts of Armenia which had been part of Russia from 1878 until World War I. From 1945 onwards, Armenians from abroad were encouraged to return home with promises of special concessions and privileges. An election to the vacant Supreme Pontificate of Holy Echmiadzin (in Soviet Armenia) was held with participation of Armenian delegates from all over the world. The growth of Armenian industry was fostered by building scores of modern factories and the completion of hydro-electric schemes harnessing Armenia's fast-flowing rivers.[10]

Immediately after 1945, conditions were harsh. Many immigrants regretted their decision to return home. But during the 1950s, Soviet Armenia really 'took off' in terms of economic growth and social improvement. In addition to natural increase through a healthy birth-rate and improved medical care, Armenians returned home from Turkey, Persia and the Lebanon – even a few from the United States. The following figures[11] speak for themselves:

**Population of Soviet Armenia**

| | |
|---|---|
| 1940 | 1,320,000 |
| 1959 | 1,763,000 |
| 1966 | 2,239,000 |
| 1970 | 2,492,000 |
| 1979 | 3,031,000 |
| 1985 | 3,317,000 |

The Armenian ethnic majority in the population is almost 90%, significant minorities being Azerbaijan or Azeri Tatars, and 70,000 Russians who comprise 2.3% of the population. There are also 57,000 Kurds and 6000 Assyrians. The numbers of Azeris has dropped dramatically – between 1989 and 1990 probably half of the Azeri population of around 200,000 has left, while Armenian refugees from Azerbaijan have arrived.

Particularly instructive is the rapid growth of the Soviet Armenian capital, Yerevan, which began life over 2750 years ago as the fortress of Erebuni, a citadel of the Urartian kings.

**Population of Yerevan**

| | |
|---|---|
| 1917 | 34,000 |
| 1926 | 65,000 |
| 1939 | 204,000 |
| 1970 | 767,000 |
| 1979 | 1,019,000 |
| 1985 | 1,148,000 |

From this, it can be seen that Yerevan now contains over a third of the entire population of the Armenian SSR. This rapid urban growth reflects the world-wide drift of rural farmers into big cities, resulting from industrialization and the search for town comforts and amenities. This somewhat artificial situation in Armenia also results from deliberate concentration of industry in the capital, and from the stony, inhospitable character of much of the countryside. Armenian industry would hardly be viable without investment made by Moscow, products of Armenian factories could only be sold with difficulty without access to the vast Soviet market; both the urban and the rural population might starve without imports of wheat from the Ukraine and the interdependence of other soviet republics.

## The perestroika era

Perestroika and glasnost found Soviet Armenia unprepared when these concepts emerged in Soviet discourse in 1985. For over a year there was virtually no change. Then the new situation manifested itself in two different but interconnected ways. One was an attack on the ossified party structure in Armenia, which had hitherto been underpinned by an elaborate system of bribes. Changes in the party apparatus began in early 1987, and accelerated with the territorial dispute over two erstwhile Armenian territories, now part of Azerbaijan SSR. As a result of nationalist confrontations, by May 1988 the former Brezhnevite leader in Armenia had been ousted and replaced by Suren Harutiunian, who held power until April 1990. Other ideas, most notably the Green struggle to clean up industrial pollution, and to end nuclear power generation in Armenia (an earthquake zone) stimulated ideas of political and economic change.

The other manifestation of perestroika was a demand for the retrocession to Armenia of one, and possibly two, territories, that most Armenians considered should be part of their national homeland – Nakhichevan and Mountainous Karabagh. While both territories were relatively small in population (267,000 and 160,000, respectively) discrimination against Armenians there has been far reaching and wideranging. Here the Armenians have not yet been successful; for the unspoken theme of perestroika has been that issues relating to nationalities and territory are off-limits.

Nakhichevan, an enclave on the southern borders with Iran, and since 1932, with Turkey, had been disputed between Armenia and Azerbaijan during the brief period of Armenian independence (1918-20) but despite an apparent surrender of Azerbaijan's claims in 1920, it never became part of Soviet Armenia. It became the subject of a clause in the bilateral treaty signed between Kemalist Turkey and the Soviet state in March 1921, which laid down that Nakhichevan would remain part of Azerbaijan and that its status could not be altered without the agreement of Turkey.

Nakhichevan in recent times has scarcely had an Armenian majority – at the time of sovietization, Armenians constituted about 40% of the population which was otherwise not homogenous, consisting of Kurds and Turko-Tatars – yet in the succeeding 70 years of Communist rule during which local rulers instituted an anti-Armenian policy this was reduced to 5% and is currently less than 2%. The population density of the 5500 sq. km. Nakhichevan ASSR is only about half that for the Armenian SSR. The population density of the Armenian SSR averages 102 per sq. km.

### Population of Nakhichevan ASSR

| | |
|---|---|
| 1940 | 131,000 |
| 1970 | 202,000 |
| 1979 | 239,000 |
| 1985 | 267,000 |

Thus the population explosion in Soviet Armenia may lead to renewed pressure for union with the Nakhichevan ASSR, as it has in respect of the predominantly Armenian Mountainous Karabagh *oblast* where the Armenian population remains in a majority.

### Political changes within Armenia

The Karabagh issue has been the most significant in Armenia and has acted as catalyst for the changes that occured within the republic itself. Gradually the old Communist-KGB structure has crumbled. However, the new Gorbachevian order, initially regarded with favour, was soon seen by Armenians as without principles. One result has been that the Armenians have sought to create their own political institutions, one of the earliest being the Karabagh Committee, an unofficial grouping created in 1988 to press for the return of Karabagh to Armenia. Leading members of the Committee were jailed by the Soviet authorities in the turbulent aftermath of the Armenian earthquake and were not released until summer 1989. However, they were not broken by this experience and it is significant that one of their number, Levon Ter-Petrosian, became President of Armenia in August 1990. On the negative side, it has to be said that the Armenian voice in defence of Karabagh was sometimes muffled and confused, expressed in turgid rhetoric in which the essential strength and simplicity of the Karabagh claim, based on democratic choice and human rights, was lost.

Further violence towards Armenians occurred in Baku in January 1990. The Azeris set upon the minority Armenian community in the city with brutal determination, killing scores, and resulting in a massive exodus of Armenian refugees attempting to escape the violence. After seven days of this brutality the Soviet army entered Baku, but its subsequent actions showed the Kremlin's desire was more to suppress the Azerbaijani Popular Front than to protect the Armenians, who were left as defenceless as before. The effect of these events on Armenian opinion has been to turn it strongly against Moscow and the Communist Party establishment. Since the summer of 1989 Azerbaijan has imposed a food and fuel blockade of Armenia itself. This has resulted in serious shortages since Armenia receives 85% of its supplies via Azerbaijan and a mere 15% through Georgia.

A dangerous manifestation of Armenian disillusion was the growth of militias in Armenia. These grew rapidly following the events in Baku, and by the summer of 1990 some 10,000 men were members of unofficial Armenian militias. They obtained most of their weapons by looting Soviet barracks. Gorbachev issued several fruitless demands for them to disband, but they, seeing the denial of the rule of law and unprotectedness that perestroika had brought them, refused to do so. Only the emergence of Ter-Petrosian's non-Communist administration has begun to bring the militias under control.

Ter-Petrosian was elected to the position of President by the Armenian Parliament, following the elections of May-August 1990. These elections provided a working majority of 35% for the All-Armenian National Movement (*Hai Hamazgain Sharzhoum*). Ter-Petrosian was elected by almost two-thirds of the parliamentary deputies. It appears that Ter-Petrosian and his mild but firm, non-adventurist, non-ideological, non-Communist administration, is seen as the best hope for Armenia. It was clear that Communism could no longer work in the republic, since it had failed to protect Armenians, to break the blockade or to grant democracy in Karabagh. Nor do Gorbachev's proposed reforms appeal to most Armenians. In August 1990 the Armenian SSR became the Republic of Armenia and declared itself a sovereign nation.

## The future for the Republic of Armenia

The Republic of Armenia still faces serious problems. Some are political and economic; how to break the continuing Azeri blockade; how to gain supplies (especially food and gas) for the severe winter; how to bring democracy, if not unity, for Karabagh; how to stave off the prospect of civil war. In addition there are new issues of international relations. Armenia must negotiate reasonable treaties with neighbouring states. Of the four states which border Armenia, Azerbaijan, in view of the virtual state of war between the two, and Turkey, with its long and continuing anti-Armenian ideology, will prove most difficult. Georgia, in theory, should be the least problematic but the election in October 1990 of Zviad Gamsakhurdia as President does not hold out the hope for easy relations, since he has accused the head of the Armenian Church of plotting to annex southern Georgia. Only Iran promises to offer anything like normal diplomatic relations to the Armenian republic. Some sort of a new treaty will need to be negotiated with Moscow. Not all of Armenia's connection with Russia, or even with Soviet Communism, has been as bad as the years 1988-90 have been. Soviet Russia built factories in Armenia, it educated the people and gave them skills, it modernized the country and gave it roads. There is hope that at some future date a government in Moscow will show an attitude to Armenia different from that of Gorbachev.

There is a danger that in the interim Armenia will hanker after unrealistic relations with overseas powers, in particular to reactivate sentimental relations with the USA or France. (It is unlikely to be with the UK, which for the past 150 years has usually been pro-Turk in its policies.) The Republic of Armenia should seek new relationships in the world arena rather than search for alliances with Western powers, a dangerous trap since post-Napoleonic history shows that great powers will always sell out Armenia at a whisper from one of her large or well-placed adversaries. Armenia certainly needs a seat at the UN as soon as possible, and beyond this should seek to negotiate alliances with her immediate neighbours, in the long term a much more secure guarantee for the safety of the Armenian people.

## Armenians in the USSR

In Armenia, the Armenians themselves therefore now number a little over three million. But it should not be forgotten that perhaps one third of the Armenians in the USSR live outside Soviet Armenia. There are substantial Armenian groups in other republics and regions. For example, the communities in Georgia alone numbered about 450,000 and in Azerbaijan the numbers were around 475,000, until the events of 1989.

Armenians of ability enjoy considerable opportunities for promotion in the USSR, since they can (or could) compete for jobs in a vast labour and economic market of some 250 million people. The late Academician I.A. Orbeli became Director of the Hermitage Museum in Leningrad, and his brother Levon was Director of the Institute of Physiology named after Pavlov. The names of Academicians Arzumanian, Knunyants, Sisakyan and Alikhanov also won international renown. In music, there is the fame and popularity of the composer Aram Khatchaturian and of the Komitas String Quartet of Yerevan.

In the USSR, Armenians are found in most major cities and are prominent in all professions, in the arts and sciences, and in trade and industry. The communities in Moscow, Nor Nakhichevan (near Rostov) and Astrakhan have a long and chequered history. The Lazarev Institute in Moscow was founded by a wealthy Armenian family in 1815; the original edifice still stands, in the Armyansky Pereulok. It now acts as the Embassy of Armenia. The Soviet motor industry in Central Asia owes much to Armenian mechanics and engineers, centred in the town of Ashkhabad. Armenian doctors and dentists are outstanding in the otherwise backward Soviet medical profession. However, there are exceptions to the rule, and an Armenian psychiatrist became notorious for promoting the detention of Soviet dissidents in mental hospitals and injecting them with harmful drugs.

The future for USSR Armenians outside the Republic of Armenia should, by virtue of their skills and experience, be an assured one. But, as with other ethnic groups, much depends on the future arrangements negotiated between the centre and the various republics, on such matters as citizenship, residence permits, availability of housing and professional qualifications. Many Armenians have built careers outside their homeland and may not wish to return on a permanent basis. Others may return, either through choice or because they feel that they have no future in other republics.

Ironically, it is in Armenia's neighbouring republics of Georgia and Azerbaijan where Armenians have felt most threatened. Georgia, in theory, should be a secure haven because of the long-standing of its Armenian community, but the October 1990 election of the veteran Georgian nationalist Zviad Gamsakhurdia as President does not promise a harmonious relationship between the Georgian majority and the Armenian minority.

Azerbaijan has become an Armenian disaster area. The Armenian community has suffered a devastating blow. By the end of 1990, 230,000 Armenians from Baku had fled to Armenia; thousands of others were in Moscow and other Soviet cities, many living with friends and family, others squatting without permits. Added to the Armenians who are still homeless after the December 1988 earthquake, they add to the already heavy burden on the new Armenian government.

# 8

## KARABAGH IN OUTLINE

'Nationalist Unrest Erupts in Armenia,' ran a headline in *Financial Times* in February 1988. The smallest republic the USSR, constituting all that remains of historic Armeni was at that time in the grip of an unprecedented wave of vast demoi strations. Hundreds of thousands of people were participating daily i nationalist rallies in Yerevan, Armenia's capital. The USSR had claimec to have solved, peacefully and for ever, the nationality problem – the problem of the status of non-Russian people within the Soviet state. These events – in Armenia and other republics – showed that claim to be premature. Gorbachev's reforms had clearly made possible the awakening that was taking place in Armenia. Perestroika and glasnost had made the unsayable sayable; until late 1987 any serious talk about nationality issues in the USSR had been virtually unsayable. As the events occurred, they were seen also to have a dark side: they were accompanied by anti-Armenian pogroms, inaccurately described, both in the USSR and the West, as 'inter-ethnic clashes'. These pogroms, perpetrated by Azeri Turks, revived memories of the 1915 genocide of Armenians, which had destroyed one third of the Armenian people, and driven another third into exile. Moreover, although under the regime of glasnost, disputes between nationalities were to some extent aired and discussed, the Armenians learnt with bitter experience that no actual change was permissable, and that the situation on the ground, far from improving, was to grow steadily worse.

Why did this sudden explosion occur? The main reason was the existence of a small mountainous territory (4388 sq. km. or 1694 sq. miles; smaller than Northumberland, larger than Essex or Kent) which was to figure in many of the headlines: Karabagh (known in Russian as Karabakh). This name is Turkish and Iranian: *kara* is Turkish for 'black', and *bagh* is Iranian for 'garden'. Sometimes it is referred to as Mountainous (in Russian, Nagorno) Karabagh. The name 'Karabagh' probably refers to the rich, laval, fertile earth that is prevalent there.[12] The region is administered by a Turkish-speaking Soviet republic, Azerbaijan. But its people are Armenian: they have no doubts about their own identity, and their language is quite clearly Armenian, albeit a dialect form. Geographically, Karabagh is the easternmost outpost of the Armenian plateau, and it was known in medieval times as the Armenian province of Artsakh. Fifteen hundred ancient Armenian buildings – churches and monasteries, built in a recognizable Armenian style – lie in its remote and beautiful hills. It was cynically attached to Azerbaijan in 1921 by Stalin; since then, the people of the province have yearned for the region's reunification to Armenia. Some notable Armenian figures have been born there, and many leading Armenian families (such as the Nubar family, prominent in 19th Century Egypt) derive originally from Karabagh. In the 18th Century, the people formed armies and local self-defence forces which acted against the incursions of various Ottoman Turkish pashas and their armies.

Karabagh, or to give its Armenian name, Artsakh, has been synonymous with struggle and warfare for centuries. The reasons are several. In the first place the district is mountainous, and mountain people have always jealously guarded their identity against the invasions of the plains-people. Islamic empires might conquer and convert the plains-dwellers, but the mountaineers were tougher. In the Armenian world, similar factors were in operation in other mountainous regions, such as Sasun and Zeitun. Here too Armenians held on to their national identity, and elements of the old social order remained until the modern period, despite conquest by foreign empires.

Secondly, there is a socio-economic reason. The mountain people of Karabagh are subsistence farmers and villagers, but for several centuries the Muslim-Tatar herdsmen of the Mughan steppe, the plain to the east of Karabagh, have habitually used the mountainous region as pasture in summer, a time of year when the lowland steppe becomes hot and malarial. Karabagh, despite its Armenian settled population, thereby became linked to Islamic economic systems.

Thirdly, there is a tendency to deny the reality of the fact that the Armenians of Karabagh are actually Armenians, but to see them as descendants of Caucasian Albanians, a people of eastern Transcaucasia who disappeared from history some time in the 11th Century. Casuists argue today that, since Soviet Azerbaijan is the successor-state to Caucasian Albania, and since (as they shakily claim) the people of Artsakh are not Armenians but are ethnically Caucasian Albanians, therefore the region should indeed be ruled by Azerbaijan and not by Armenia.

Fourthly, the administrative divisions which Imperial Russia gave to the region (which it captured from the Persian Qajar empire in 1805) meant that it was, from that time up to the collapse of the Russian Empire in 1917, linked administratively to the non-Armenian hinterland, and not to the Armenian region of Yerevan and Nakhichevan. Fifthly, in more recent times, Karabagh has been seen as a factor in the struggle for the survival of the Armenian people, threatened by the aggressive ideology of pan-Turkism, which seeks to impose a Turkic identity on virtually the entire region, and to deny the reality of anything non-Turkish there, as a prelude to the political link-up of all Turkish (and less than Turkish) lands.

It is true that (sixthly) the Armenians of Karabagh, like all Armenians, are Christian, and the Azerbaijanis or Tatars are Muslim; but the religious distinction has never been of great significance and it should not be overestimated. Religion has seldom been a seriously divisive issue in Transcaucasia, even in times of great upheaval such as 1905, when the whole of the region was rent with revolution and ethnic violence.

There is perhaps a seventh element too: that Armenia, which is within the USSR, is on the frontier with Turkey, which is a member of Nato and the Council of Europe. Turkey's ethno-linguistic cousins are the rulers of Baku, not the peasantry of Artsakh, and so Turkish, and Nato, and perhaps Western sentiment in general, may tend to side with the oppressors rather than with the oppressed. But with the ending of the Cold War, these distinctions and rigidly held attitudes have become somewhat blurred. However, it is one of the bitter facts of diplomatic history that great powers have almost always tended to forge alliances with the large and well-placed neighbours of Armenians, and to overlook rights and justice where they concern Armenians.

## Three meanings of 'Karabagh'

The name 'Karabagh' has been in use since the 14th Century. It has three different meanings, so there can be confusion.

Initially, it denoted much of the plain as well as the mountainous region: approximately the Armenian provinces of Artsakh and Utik, which lay between Lake Sevan, the River Kura and the River Araxes. Until the 5th Century AD these provinces had been part of Great Armenia[13]; thereafter they became attached to the Persian province of Arran, or Caucasian Albania (which has no relationship with European Albania). In successive centuries their rulers changed: Arabs, Seljuk Turks, Mongols, Turkmens, Ottoman Turks, Safavid Persians and, finally, Russians.

Secondly, 'Mountainous Karabagh' denotes the region south-east of Lake Sevan, minus the plains and the region of Zangezur. It takes in the present-day contested regions of Shahumian and Getashen, sites of

Armenian villages in Azerbaijan, which have been blockaded for much of 1989 and 1990. Thirdly, the official Soviet territory of the 'Nagorno Karabakh Autonomous *Oblast* [region]', or NKAO for short, encompasses a smaller area still, 4388 sq. km. (1694 sq. miles)

## Karabagh in outline

The people of the highland region speak (for the most part) an eastern dialect of Armenian, whereas the lowlanders, known formerly as Tatars or Tartars, and now as Azeris or Azerbaijanis, speak Azeri, one of the Turkic family of languages.

There are two major mountain ranges in the Autonomous Region, the Murovdag range to the north and the Karabagh range to the south (with maximum heights of 3724 metres – 12215 feet, and 2725 metres – 8938 feet, respectively). To the north-east and east, the plains slope into Azerbaijan. The region is noted for its mineral deposits of various ores, marble, Iceland spar and graphite and is also rich in mineral springs. The climate is moderate, with dry winters. The January temperature in the plain region seldom falls below -2 C, in the mountains -10 C. Summers are similarly moderate, the July temperature rarely reaching above 25 C. Spring and summer precipitation is quite high: annual rainfall in the plain is 400-600 mm. and in the mountains 800 mm. The rivers flow through deep gorges, and they have in places been harnessed for irrigation and power generation. There is a hydro-electric power station on the Terter river.

The total 1976 population of the Nagorno Karabagh Autonomous Oblast was 157,200, which gave a ratio of 35 persons per sq. km. Of that population, 81% were Armenians, 18% Azeris and 1% Russians. There are two cities, Stepanakert (formerly Khankend) and Shushi (or Shusha). Twenty one percent of the population was at that time employed in industry and construction, whereas 45% were in agriculture. Industry is small scale – food processing, silk and footwear manufacture; there are garment and furniture factories in Stepanakert. Agriculture is intensive, and diversified. Karabagh wine is very distinctive, a rich, dark, herby drink; in the 1970s the state farms were producing 34,000 tonnes of grapes per annum. Fruit, grain and cotton are also grown and perennial planting allows the production of winter wheat. Tobacco is also grown in the north-eastern district of NKAO. The region is also important for meat and dairy products: sheep, cattle and pigs are raised. The climate also supports the growth of mulberries, making possible the silk-weaving industry: Karabagh carpets have been well-known for centuries.

# 9

## ANCIENT AND MEDIEVAL KARABAGH

### The eastern provinces of Armenia before the 5th Century

The earliest historical evidence on this region of Transcaucasia dates from the Urartu period (9th-6th Century BC). The province of Urtekhe or Urtekhini[14] at that time formed part of the territory conquered in the 8th Century BC by the Urartian kings who, from their capital Tushpa or Van, in Western Armenia, extended their domain northeastward to Transcaucasian Armenia. The name Urtekhe is the verbal ancestor of the Armenian name Artsakh, which appears to be connected with the name Orkhistena given to it by the Greek geographer Strabo.[15] After the fall of Urartu (6th Century) this region passed under the domination of the Medes and the Achaemenid Persians.

The Armenian historian Movses Khorenatsi (5th-8th Century AD) states that the province of Utik (together with that of Artsakh adjoining it to the south) formed part, in the 4th-2nd Centuries BC of the Armenian kingdom of the Ervanduni, otherwise known as the Orontids.[16] Some writers are of the opinion that, when the King Artashes (189-160 BC) completed the reunification of the kingdom of Greater Armenia, some Caucasian tribes living in Artsakh and Utik were forcibly attached to it. However, Strabo, on whose evidence this theory is based, when describing the conquests made at the expense of the Medes and Iberians (Georgians today), does not mention either Artsakh or Utik, probably since these provinces already formed an integral part of Armenia.

At all events, Strabo states that, in the 2nd Century BC, the population living in Greater Armenia (including Artsakh and Utik) all spoke the same language (ie. Armenian).[17] Strabo also indicates that the eastern regions were economically prosperous and militarily powerful, since they provided the king of Armenia with the most cavalry.

The eastern provinces of Artsakh and Utik were converted to Christianity like the rest of the country at the beginning of the 4th Century, and they remained within the kingdom of Armenia until its fall in 428 AD. Historians of the Baku school have attempted to show that in ancient and medieval times, the territory between Lake Sevan and the Kura belonged not to Armenia but to Caucasian Albania which, according to their theory, was the direct ancestor of modern Azerbaijan.[18]  However, many Greek and Roman authors (Strabo, 1st Century BC to 1st Century AD; Pliny (the Elder), 1st Century AD; Plutarch, 1st-2nd Century AD; Ptolemy, 2nd Century AD; Dio Cassius, 2nd-3rd Century AD), point out that until the 5th Century AD, the two provinces belonged to Armenians and that the Kura river marked the northern frontier of Armenia. Armenian sources make the same point, especially Agathangelos, Pavstos Buzand, of the 5th Century; the atlas known as 'Ashkharhatsouits', of the 7th Century. The Kura river separated Armenia from Caucasian Albania.[19]

## Artsakh and Utik Separate from Armenia

In 385 or 387 AD, Armenia was partitioned between the Roman Empire (soon to be Byzantium), and Persia. In 428, the Sasanid Persians put an end to the existence of the kingdom of Armenia and divided the region into three new administrative units. This was the beginning of an era during which Artsakh and Utik were cut off politically from Armenia, and annexed to another unit. The whole of the eastern part of the region was reorganized into a new province (*marzpanat*), called Arran or Albania (Aghvank, Alvank, or Aghouank in Armenian). This included, between the Caucasus mountains and the Kura, the kingdom of Albania and the ethnic groups bordering the Caspian Sea; and also between the Kura and Araxes rivers and Lake Sevan, the two territories detached from Armenia: Artsakh and Utik. This new unit was probably constituted around the middle of the 5th Century.[20]

The territory known as Albania shifted south-westward. The political units lying to the east, along the banks of the Caspian, broke away, ceasing to call themselves Albanians. On the other hand, the Christian kingdom of Caucasian Albania, which the Persians tolerated until 461, was enlarged on the west to include a part of Armenia in which Albanian influence was strong. As a result, there was formed a new Caucasian Albania, in which the provinces of Artsakh and Utik came to play a preponderant role: the Albanian capital was transferred to Partav (Bardhaa), in Utik, at the beginning of the 6th Century. It was probably because Utik was more homogeneous and more highly developed than the tribes living on the north bank of the Kura that the Armenian population imposed its language and its culture.

At the time of the Armenian hero Vardan, and his successors (second half of the 5th Century), Sasanid Persia attempted to convert both Armenia and the region to the east of it to Mazdaism or worship of the sacred elements of earth, air, fire and water. Albania played an important part in this campaign, contributing its cavalry, and providing the Armenian troops with a base. The Persians had set up an Arsacid dynasty in Albania, but there also existed local princes, Armenians belonging to the Arranshahik family. One member of this family, Vatchagan the Pious, took advantage of a weakening in Sasanid authority, at the end of the 5th and beginning of the 6th Century, to re-establish the kingdom of west Albania on the Artsakh and Utik territories and on the northern bank of the Kura.[21] The country then went through a period of intense development, building as many churches as there are days in the year,[22] many of which formed the basis for large monastic centres which lasted throughout the medieval period.

Caucasian Albania had been converted to Christianity at the beginning of the 4th Century by St. Gregory the Illuminator, who came from Armenia and appointed Thomas as bishop. Around the year 330, Grigoris, the grandson of St. Gregory, who was already in charge of the eastern provinces of Armenia, was in turn appointed bishop of the kingdom of Albania. The oldest church of this region is to be found in present-day Mountainous Karabagh: the church of the monastery of Amaras established by St. Gregory and completed by St. Grigoris. Here St. Grigoris was buried in 338, and on his tomb King Vatchagan the Pious erected in 489 a funerary chapel (which it is still possible to visit).[23] Tradition has it that this same monastery housed the first school in Artsakh, opened at the beginning of the 5th Century by the inventor of the Armenian alphabet, Mesrop Mashtots. In view of this ecclesiastical connection with Armenia, it was natural that the Albanian church should be subordinated to the church of Armenia, which it joined, at the Councils of Dvin (6th Century) in repudiating the dogma of the Council of Chalcedon, which was seen as dyophysite, or attributing two natures to Christ, and moving away from Greek Orthodoxy. In 552, the seat of the Albanian Church was transferred from Derbent or Darband (in present-day Daghestan), to Partav (or Bardhaa).

As part of the politico-geographical shift previously mentioned, this transfer accentuated the Armenian influence; and one of its consequences was that the Armenian language supplanted Caucasian Albanian as the language of the church and the state. The Albanian language, although provided with an alphabet by Mesrop Mashtots, died out. (The sole surviving traces of the Albanian language are a few fragments of inscriptions dating from the 6th and 7th Centuries, most of them found near Minguechaur, on the north bank of the Kura.)[24] For the 7th-8th Centuries there is interesting evidence of an Armenian dialect being spoken by the inhabitants of Artsakh: the Armenian author Stepannos Siunetsi, in a grammar manual, advises people who want to learn the Armenian language to study its 'peripheric dialects', including 'Artsakhian'. This advice again is quoted, in the 14th Century, by the scholar Essayi Nchetsi.[25]

The Arabs, after conquering the region in the 7th-8th Centuries, formed a vast administrative unit which they named Arminiyya, covering Armenia, part of Georgia and Arran (Albania) stretching to the shores of the Caspian Sea.

## Continuation of the 'Albanian Episode'

In 9th Century Armenia, when the Arab domination weakened, Armenian princes from the Bagratuni family began to reinforce their positions and to extend their possessions. In the east, paradoxically, whilst Albania was becoming increasingly Armenian, the Armenian elite of Artsakh and Utik adopted a form of 'Albanian' patriotism, and they used this 'ideology' to reinforce their centrifugal tendencies, designed to counteract – as in the other large Armenian provinces, such as Vaspurakan and Siunik – the centralizing policy of the Bagratid authorities.[26] The descendants of the Arranshahiks, in the 9th-10th Centuries, assumed royal power. They set up, on their Artsakh territories (present-day Karabagh) the two kingdoms of Dizak and Khachen (the latter including a part of Siunik, now the south-east of the Armenian SSR), which were recognized by both the Arabs and the Byzantines.[27] These units were subsequently integrated as vassal states in the Bagratid kingdom of Armenia. It is interesting to note that the Byzantine emperor Constantine Porphyrogenitus mentioned amongst the Armenian political figures with whom he corresponded 'the prince of Khachen in Armenia'.[28]

The best picture of this Armeno-Albanian identity is given by the Albanian historian Movses Daskhurantsi. In his 'History of the Aghvank' ('History of Albania'), written (in Armenian) about 980, he speaks with enthusiasm of the past of his country; stressing its close links with Armenia but, at the same time, setting out to prove the great age of the Albanian church, and its right to independence.[29] Dealing mainly with the Armenian part of the country, Movses Daskhurantsi says nothing about the Islamicization of the east of ancient Albania, described in 10th Century Arab documents.[30] Eastern Albania, after the disappearance of its Christian kingdoms, gradually ceased to exist as such, some of its population was partially assimilated (in the western regions) to the Armenians and the Georgians; but the majority was converted to Islam through mixing with the Arabs, and later the Turks. This Islamicized Caucasian substratum, with the addition of Iranian and, in particular, Turkish elements gave birth to the Azeri ethnic group, at one time called Tatars, of Turkish language and Shii Muslim religion, which today forms the bulk of the population of Azerbaijan.

Such was the end of the 'Albanian episode' of the history of the eastern provinces of Armenia. After the Seljuk invasion (in the second half of the 11th Century) and the fall of the Christian kingdoms, these regions continued to shelter Armenian princes, heirs of the Arranshahiks who returned to the Armenian orbit and flourished during the 13th Century. Armenian historians sometimes continued to use the term Albania, not meaning a distinct political unit, in reference to the provinces of Artsakh and Utik. The term 'Albanian' around the year 1000 AD only described the Christians of ancient Caucasian Albania, ie. the Armenians and descendants of Albanians most of whom were Armenized. However, it took on an ecclesiastical meaning.[31] It continued to be applied to the patriarchate in charge of the Armenians of present-day Azerbaijan. This patriarchate had its seat in the monastery of Gandzasar in Artsakh (Mountainous Karabagh) and, until the 19th Century, bore the title of Catholicosate of Albania.

This illustrates the complexity of the respective terms 'Albanian' and 'Armenian', and explains why it is essential to exercise care in their use. It is, therefore, unfortunate when, because of political considerations, these complex terms are carelessly used. Thus, for instance, the Baku historians strive to minimize and denigrate the Armenian element in Albania, a country which they say, always existed, and formed the immediate predecessor of present-day Azerbaijan.[32] If the Baku school theory is accepted, it is hard to account for the national spirit which inspired and continues to inspire the Armenians of the Albanian region. Moreover, it makes it hard to explain the thousands of works of art and culture created here, the 1500 Armenian architectural monuments to be found in Mountainous Karabagh. It is claimed by the Baku historians to be all a matter of deception, forced assimilation and manipulation. It is possible to perceive the purpose of such an interpretation: to show that these peoples' link with Armenia has no historical basis, since they are in fact Albanians, in other words Azerbaijanis; to prove that the Armenian character of Mountainous Karabagh is a myth, and that the 'Albanians' living there have no grounds for declaring that they do not belong to the Republic of Azerbaijan.

## The great feudal families

In the 12th Century, the former Artsakh, henceforth more often known by the name of Khachen, was divided up between three prince-ly families, descendants of the Arranshahik dynasty. At the end of the 11th Century, these families entered the service of the Zakarian princes, Armenian dignitaries at the Georgian court, and the liberators of Armenia, hitherto occupied by the Seljuks.[33] Among these families one, that of Prince Hassan Jalal Dawla (1214-1261), later known as Jalalian, who reigned over a large part of Khachen, attaining a certain degree of power and independence: Prince Hassan (the use of Arab first names was at that time fairly common amongst the Armenians) was one of the main figures of Armenian political and cultural life. After trying in vain to fight the Mongols, Hassan contrived to win their favour and maintained good relations with them. He made two jour-neys to Karakorum, acting as the representative of the whole of Arme-nia, and obtained from the Great Khan certain privileges amounting to autonomy.[34] He promoted an agreement between the Armenian King-dom of Cilicia and the Mongols. Hassan Jalal, proclaimed in certain sources and inscriptions as 'autocratic lord of Khachen, prince of princes, King of Aghvank, King of the land of Artsakh', was also a great builder, not only in Khachen (eg. the churches of Gandzasar and Vat-jarr), but also in the centre of eastern Armenia where, in 1248, he was responsible for the restoration of the monastery of Kecharris.

The history of the Jalalian family and their architectural and artistic work is documented in the Armenian inscriptions on the walls of the many monuments erected in Khachen during the flourishing period of the 13th Century.[35] The fine monastery of Gandzasar, built between 1216 and 1261 near the Jalalian residence, was one of the temporal and spiritual centres of the principality. Attached in theory to the pri-matial catholicossate of Armenia, it was used from the 14th Century until 1815 as the seat of the 'catholicossate of Albania', henceforth occupied by members of the Jalalian family. The monastery of Gandza-sar is characterized by a richly carved decoration with several portraits of the patron princes. This monastery has one of the finest specimens of an Armenian 13th Century ante-nave with the vault resting on two pairs of intersecting arches, and having a central skylight rimmed by stalactite work.[36]

Just beyond the present north-west boundary of Mountainous Karabagh, there is another 12th-13th Century monastery, Dadivank. In fairly good condition, it comprises perhaps the largest and most com-plete monastic group of medieval Armenia, with some 20 edifices divided into three parts, used, respectively, for worship, living quarters and ancillary purposes.[37] Gandzasar and Dadivank, Gtichavank, Kha-travank, Saint James, Brri Eghtsi – like the other monasteries of Arme-nia – contained scriptoriums, where numerous manuscripts were copied and illuminated. Some of the finest *khachkars* or cross-stones of Armenia were carved at Khachen in the 13th Century. Amongst the most famous are the two at Gtichavank, carved around 1246, one of which is preserved at Echmiadzin. Mention should also be made, in order to stress the flourishing state of Khachen in the medieval era, of its many fortresses, still partially preserved: Jraberd, Khachenaberd, Dizapayt, Gaylatun and others.

## The five Armenian meliks in the medieval period

The descendants of the Jalalian family survived the invasion of Tamer-lane (end of 14th Century), the incursions of the Turkmens (15th-16th Centuries) and also the Turko-Persian wars (16th-17th Centuries). Thus Mountainous Karabagh was the only part of Armenia where a tradition of national sovereignty was preserved unbroken until the late medieval period. During the 16th-17th Centuries, there were five Armenian fam-ilies which retained power over their mountain domains in the territo-ry of the former Khachen: the five 'melikdoms' of Khamsa (*khamsa*, in Arabic means five).[38] The leading families of these provinces received their titles of *melik* (prince) in the 15th and 16th Centuries from the Turkoman rulers. They were confirmed by Shah Abbas of Persia, in 1603. Officially they became attached to the Persian province admin-istered from Gandzak; however, they were largely autonomous in mat-ters of defence and internal policy, justice and taxation.

Armenia, partitioned between two empires (Turkey and Persia) had long since lost its sovereignty and ceased to be able to protect its popu-lation, and the meliks were the sole authorities capable of withstand-ing threats from abroad and maintaining national traditions. It is understandable, therefore, that Karabagh, where the leading families survived until modern times, should have become an important exam-ple of national identity: it has been described as 'the bastion of Arme-nian political and cultural consciousness'.[39]

It was in the five melikdoms and in the neighbouring province of Siunik that there arose, in the 17th-18th Centuries together with the desire for a national renaissance, the idea of recreating an independent national state, allied to Georgia and protected by Russia. Diplomatic steps to this effect were taken in the 18th Century by three Armenians: Israel Ori, Bishop Minas and the Catholicos Essayi Hassan-Jalalian.

They approached the West European, Russian and Georgian authorities with a view to freeing Armenia from the Turks and Persians. At the same time, they coordinated their military capability in Siunik under Davit Bek, a remarkable leader. The monastery of Gandzasar formed the organizational centre of this political and military activity, which Russia half-encouraged, holding out the prospect of the creation of a 'Christian' Armenian state.

During the first half of the 18th Century, 10,000 men, led by the *yuzbashis* ('commanders'; the word is Turkish) of the five melikdoms, held off the Turkish and Persian troops in hoping for the advance of the Russian army of Peter the Great. Some of them entered the service of Iran in order to fight the Turks. Encouraged by the Caucasian campaign of Peter the Great, who had reached Derbent and Baku in 1722, Karabagh and Siunik rose in arms against the Persian occupation and, in the 1720s, enjoyed a short period of independence.[40] In order to facilitate the progress of the Russian troops, the king of Georgia, the Catholicos of Gandzasar and the meliks had even assembled, near Gandzak, an Armeno-Georgian army of 40,000 men. But the time for such a Russian advance into Transcaucasia had not yet arrived.

## The 18th Century:
## Turks become established in Mountainous Karabagh

Around 1750, disunion amongst the five Armenian lords due to the excessive ambition of one of them enabled Panah Ali Khan, the chief of a Turkish tribe, to establish himself in Khachen. Thus the khanate of Shusha, later the khanate of Karabagh, was established in the heart of the Armenian mountain stronghold, in a fortress later to become the town of Shushi or Shusha. Ibrahim Khalil, the son of Panah, gradually assumed control of the whole of what was formerly Khachen, and also of a part of the neighbouring province of Siunik without, however, succeeding in eliminating the Armenian melikdoms.

A Muslim presence had already existed, since the 10th Century, along the northern and south-eastern borders of Karabagh, as the result of the establishment of Shaddadid Kurdish emirs in the town of Gandzak (formerly in Utik; it has alternately been known as Ganja, then Elizavetpol, then Kirovabad) and also on the Mughan plain. After the Seljuk invasion, a Turkish tribe, the Oghuz, in the 11th-12th Centuries gradually occupied the former Albania or Arran. They imposed their language but did not manage to penetrate into the Armenian mountains.[41] In the 16th Century, there were reported to be living on the Mughan plain 24 Kurdish and 32 Turkish tribes, the principal of which was the Jevanchir tribe[42] which came into conflict with Armenian movements and was conquered by Davit Bek in 1722. It was thus not until after the 1750s that the Turkish Muslim element known as the Tatars or Azeris, became established in Shushi, in the heart of the former Khachen. At the same time, a part of the Armenian population of the far north of the region (in the melikdoms of Jiraberd and Gulistan) emigrated to Georgia.

Despite these shifts, the number of Muslims in Mountainous Karabagh was small. It is known that the population of Karabagh was Armenian, as witnessed throughout the whole of the medieval period (a Persian geographer, in the 13th Century, wrote that 'the population is Armenian', and a German traveller, Johann Schiltberger, in the 15th Century, stated clearly that: 'Karabagh is situated in Armenia').[43] Its population remained largely Armenian at the end of the 18th Century, a fact confirmed by the official Turkish, Georgian and Russian documents of the time. General Potemkin wrote in 1793, in a report to the Empress Catherine II about the submission of Ibrahim Khan: 'As soon as the occasion arises, we must consider the question of putting the administration of this region, which is inhabited by Armenians, under the charge of a national and so re-establishing in Asia a Christian state, in accordance with the august promises of your imperial highness, made through my intermediary, to the Armenian meliks'.[44] A decree of Tsar Paul I stated that, in 1797, the Armenian population of the region numbered 11,000 families. And lastly, at the beginning of the 20th Century, there were in the Armenian bishopric of Karabagh, 222 churches serving more than 200,000 parishioners. The percentage of Muslims at that time was not more than 5%.

# 10

## RUSSIA AND KARABAGH: 1805-1918

### The 19th Century: Russia enters Karabagh

U nstable conditions in the second half of the 18th Century led the Catholicoses of Gandzasar and the leading families of Armenia to look to Russia. The Khan of Karabagh turned for support to Ottoman Turkey. At the beginning of the 19th Century, Russia launched an attack on the Persian Empire in Transcaucasia; and in 1805 Russia took over Karabagh. Her conquest was confirmed by the Russo-Persian peace treaty concluded at Gulistan in 1813.[45] The year 1822 saw the disappearance of both the Armenian meliks and the Khanate of Karabagh, which was transformed into a Russian province. With a view to neutralizing national claims and dividing in order the better to rule, the Russian authorities later proceeded to make several changes in the territories they had conquered.

As a result, Mountainous Karabagh, geographically an extension of the Armenian plateau, but which was conquered by Russia 21 years before the Armenian territories around Yerevan, remained separate and was attached instead to the east. In 1840 it was incorporated in the Caspian province; in 1846 it became part of Shemakha province, renamed Baku province in 1859. In 1868 it became part of Elizavetpol province. (Elizavetpol was the new name for Gandzak, or Ganja.) In this province Christian Armenians and Muslim Turks (then called Tatars) lived together, although differing in culture, language, religion and way of life. The Armenians were by tradition settled farmers and enterpreneurs, the Tatars (now known as Azeris) were originally seminomad shepherds, under leading military families who were also extensive landlords. Thus the seeds of conflict were sown.[46]

Karabagh stayed as part of the province of Elizavetpol until 1917. It was the scene, in the 19th Century, of a certain amount of intellectual and economic development, and the town of Shushi became a principal Armenian cultural centre: numerous books, and also five Armenian-language newspapers were published there; five churches were built in the 19th Century, as well as three mosques (including two in 1875

83

and 1883), the only Muslim monuments in Mountainous Karabagh.

## Russian Transcaucasia

During the early 19th Century, Russia gained a series of victories over Qajar Persia and the Ottoman Empire in the territory south of the Caucasus mountains. By 1880 the Caucasian vice-royalty included the following parts of the territory of Transcaucasia, from west to east: almost the whole of Georgia, the eastern part of Armenia (western Armenia, the major part, remained under the Ottomans) and the northern fringe of Azerbaijan. (The major part of this region, around Tabriz, was kept by the Persian Empire.)

Transcaucasia, in this form, constitutes a mosaic of populations. The Georgians are concentrated in the north and west, the Armenians exist almost everywhere with Muslim Turkish peoples, mostly Shii, who were called by the Russians 'Caucasian Tatars'. The eastern part of Karabagh is flat and peopled mainly by Tatars, nomad stockbreeders who, in summer, take their herds up into the hills, populated mostly by Armenians. Mountainous Karabagh constitutes, as it were, an advance fortress, protecting Armenia against invasion from the east.

It is clear from the map that the geographical situation of Armenia, lying across the Russo-Ottoman frontier, breaks the continuity of the Turkic world, stretching all the way from the Bosphorus to Central Asia; and this is one of the reasons why the Turks, east and west, from time to time pursue policies perhaps intended to lead to the physical elimination of the Armenians inhabiting this region; this was given new impetus by the development, at the beginning of the 20th Century, of the ideology of 'pan-Turkism' (known also as 'pan-Turanism') both in the Ottoman Empire and in Azerbaijan. The Turkish general Khalil Pasha told the Armenian leaders explicitly, in September 1918: 'We want to re-establish our links with our former territory, Turan; and for this purpose, we need a passage connecting our two countries, unhampered by foreign jurisdiction'[47]. The 'passage' in question is composed of the three districts named above, Karabagh in particular, which explains the intensive attacks on and the dogged defence of this mountain stronghold.

In this context, relations between Armenians and Tatars in Transcaucasia were bound at one level to be problematic, despite the fact that these two peoples had long lived together in the same regions, even the same towns. In the regional capital, Tiflis in Georgia, the population was preponderantly Armenian. The other large town, Baku, lying on the shore of the Caspian, owed its spectacular development to its oil, which attracted an important minority of Armenian as well as Russian, Swedish, English and other European business managers. All the other towns in the region were far smaller, few of them, at the beginning of the 20th Century, having a population of more than 20,000. They included Yerevan and Alexandropol, preponderantly Armenian, and Elizavetpol, preponderantly Tatar.

At that time, the third largest town of Transcaucasia was in Mountainous Karabagh: Shushi, with a population of around 40,000, was preponderantly Armenian. The lower town was occupied largely by Tatars, while the higher town, which was Armenian, was like a fortress.[48] Madame Chantre, who visited the town in 1890, speaks of the extremism of the Muslims of Shushi. But from 1827, with the arrival of missionaries from Basle who established a school and a printing press in the town, Shushi gradually became a flourishing centre of Armenian culture, the most important after Tiflis and Baku.[49] In addition to its schools and monuments, Shushi became after 1865 a centre for theatrical activity culminating, in 1891, in the building of a large theatre. Also, from 1874 onwards, the presses in Shushi published numerous periodicals, as well as first editions of the works of numerous authors, including those of the celebrated historian Leo, who was born as Arakel Babakhanian in Shushi in 1860. He is the author of a three-volume history of Armenia (Tiflis/Yerevan, 1917-47). In 1900, Shushi was third, after Constantinople and Tiflis, for the number of Armenian students it sent abroad.

This upsurge of Armenian culture in Karabagh was checked as a result of the evolution of Tsarist policy in the last decades of the 19th Century. As from 1868, the administrative structure of Transcaucasia was artificially changed, and eastern Armenia was cut in three: the province of Yerevan, preponderantly Armenian, included the district of Nakhichevan, but was cut off from Zangezur and from Karabagh, which formed two of the five districts of the province of Elizavetpol, a province where the Tatars constituted then, and now, a majority.

After 1881, during the reign of Alexander III, Russia looked increasingly towards Central Asia and the Far East. Its interest in Transcaucasia declined, and a new policy of seeking to avoid conflict with the Ottoman Empire, albeit in decline, naturally favoured the Tatars of Transcaucasia as opposed to the Armenians. After 1882, the title 'Viceroy' was abolished and replaced by 'Governor General', a post conferred by Nicholas II, in 1896, on one of his close friends, Prince G Golitsyn, a crude, cruel man of limited intelligence, anti-Armenian, bent on Russifying the country by force. In June 1903, after closing the Armenian schools, he decreed the confiscation of the property of the

Armenian church, provoking a popular uprising, at Shushi in particular. The Armenians, increasingly conscious of the need to organize self-defence, more particularly after the massacres in the Ottoman Empire in 1895, reacted by giving strong allegiance to the political parties, established in 1887 and 1890 with a view to bringing about change in Ottoman Armenia. They engaged in every form of action, including terrorism. Golitsyn was relieved of his office in January 1905, but the seeds of conflict were already sown in this year of 'the first Russian revolution'. What is usually known as the 'Armeno-Tatar war' was to last a year and a half, and Karabagh was to be one of the main scenes of the fighting.

### The 'Armeno-Tatar War'

It was with the acquiescence, the complicity, of the Tsarist authorities that, in February 1905, riots broke out in Baku, lasting for several days. At the beginning the Tatars were free to massacre with impunity, but the Armenian reaction came quickly, organized largely by the Dashnaks (who were at this time socialists). The number of casualties ran into hundreds on both sides. From Baku, the rioting spread to Nakhichevan, a district bordering on the Persian Empire, where there were large numbers of Tatar landowners, and where, in May 1905, many unarmed Armenians were killed.

Soon the fighting spread to Karabagh.[50] Encouraged by the fact that previous crimes had gone unpunished, the Tatars, in July, attacked a bus on the important road between Shushi and Evlakh, a station on the Batum-Baku railway line; and in August there were further similar incidents, both along this strategic road and in Shushi itself. The capital of the district was sacked and over 400 Armenian houses were burnt. But the Armenians held the approach roads and, thanks to their position in the top of the town and to their efficient preparations, they emerged victorious after five days of fighting. This 'first battle of Shushi' ended, at the end of August, in a victory for the Armenians. The skirmishes continued in September in other villages of Karabagh, with the defeat of the Tatars. The fighting then moved to the neighbouring district of Zangezur, from which a large part of the Turkish population was driven out; and then to Yerevan, at that time half-Armenian and half-Tatar.

Before this, there had been further clashes in Baku, the most spectacular and most violent of them in September.[51] Infuriated by the news from Shushi, the Muslim population of Baku attacked the Armenians and for several days a murderous battle raged in the town, ringed round by flames arising from the oil-fields, set afire throughout the whole of the region. Most of the oil wells were owned by Armenians. Considerable material damage was done, and two-thirds of the 600 or so victims were Tatars. At the end of 1905, there was a third pogrom at Baku, and the war spread to Tiflis and Elizavetpol, where the Armenians, being better organized, suffered fewer casualties than the Tatars.

The year 1905 was thus marked by successful Armenian self-defence, usually led by the Armenian Dashnak party. It was in order to try to counter the influence of the political parties that the Tsarist authorities authorized the re-opening of the schools and, in August 1905, restored their property to the clergy.[52] In 1906, there was another outbreak of violence in Karabagh. In summer, the Tatar nomads from the plain were accustomed to go up into Armenian Mountainous Karabagh with their herds. That year, the nomads were armed, and had been given instructions. They cut the roads, isolating Shushi and began to liquidate the surrounding villages, inhabited by unarmed Armenians. Meantime preparations were made in the Tatar town of Aghdam, lying on the strategic road from Shushi to Evlakh, for an attack on Shushi – part of whose population was Tatar. The Armenians avoided direct conflict. Despite the pro-Tatar attitude of the Russian authorities, the Armenians, though numerically inferior, won this 'second battle of Shushi' which 'lasted, with a few intervals, nine days, transforming the town into a veritable battlefield'.[53] The fighting came to an end on 22 July 1906.

## From 1906 to 1918

While the Armenians in Russian Armenia, and more especially in Karabagh, resisted Turkish attacks, the 'final solution' was being prepared for them in Ottoman Armenia. In this region indeed, power was in the hands of the Turks, and they were preparing for the application of the pan-Turkish theories clearly summed up by Vehib Pasha, commander of the Turkish army on the eastern front, in 1918: 'We have left the Balkans, and we are also leaving Africa, but it is our duty to spread to the east, for it is there that our blood, our faith and our language are to be found.'[54] Two Turkish parties were to govern the application of this plan; in the Ottoman Empire, the *Ittihad* or 'Committee for Union and Progress' popularly known as the Young Turks, assumed power in Constantinople in 1908, while in Russian Transcaucasia, the Tatars espoused the nationalist and pan-Islamist ideology of the *Musavat* (Equality) party, founded in 1912. Owing to its links with the Ittihad, the party often acted as a kind of agency for Turkey in Russia, cutting off Armenia, and in particular seeking mastery of the three disputed districts: Nakhichevan, Zangezur and Karabagh.

On the eve of World War I, the three main parties in Transcaucasia were the Mensheviks (for the Georgians) the Dashnak (for the Armenians) and the Musavats (for the Tatars). Bolshevism had little influence, operating mainly in Tiflis and above all in Baku, which became its main stronghold. One of its leading figures was the Armenian Stepan Shahumian, a dedicated follower of Lenin, whose popularity, however, did not equal that of another Armenian, the hero Antranig (or Andranik), an ex-Dashnak, and a remarkable organizer of guerilla warfare. The activity of this able leader was exercised on both sides of the Russo-Ottoman frontier.

Until 1918, Transcaucasia remained outside the principal zone of the World War in which the two powers administering Armenia were enemies. The Ittihad took the opportunity after 1915 to organize the genocide of the Ottoman Armenians. Then in 1917 came the Russian revolutions: first the February revolution, which was warmly greeted by Armenians, particularly because the Provisional Government recognized as Armenian several disputed areas of Transcaucasia, including Karabagh; then the October revolution. This completely changed the situation in the region. It caused the dispersal of the Russian troops, and thus opened the way for the Turkish authorities to fill the vacuum and advance in fulfilment of their the pan-Turkish aims. To this end, against the advice of their German allies, they proceeded to transfer troops from Palestine to the Caucasian front.[55]

Transcaucasia, a somewhat artificial unit composed of three different peoples, in 1917 signed a truce with Turkey. Karabagh had, since October, been *de facto* independent. A Council of Commissars reflected a hitherto unknown cohabitation of Tatars and Armenians. At Shushi there were three joint congresses in succession. Overall, a precarious peace reigned until the summer of 1918, despite sporadic clashes between Tatars and Armenians. The Armenians, looking to the future, set up an Armenian Union of Karabagh and Zangezur, under the historian Leo, designed to improve coordination between these two mountain regions, since none had any illusions about the lasting peaceful coexistence of the Tatars and Armenians. Then in the summer of 1918, the Ottoman invasion wrought havoc throughout the area.

In March 1918, while Russia, at Brest-Litovsk, was accepting the German conditions for peace, the Turkish army crossed eastward over the 1914 frontiers. The Ottoman War Minister, Enver Pasha, sent his half brother Nuri Pasha to Elizavetpol, to reinforce the Musavatist troops and form an 'army of Islam'. Mountainous Karabagh was cut off from the rest of Azerbaijan, where the Armenian villages were sacked, and their inhabitants murdered. The aim was to force the Armenians to recognize the authority of the Musavat party. During this time, the Ottoman army advanced inexorably, and seized the port of Batum where, in May, peace talks were held between a unified Turkish delegation and a Transcaucasian delegation composed of three factions having nothing in common. The visit paid on 22 May by the Ottoman Minister of the Marine (Jemal Pasha of the Ittihad party) was significant in that he treated the Tatars as brothers whom the Turks had come to rescue. He spoke very courteously to the Georgians, but told the Armenians that relations with them could only be based on hatred. There were here all the ingredients for the disintegration of the Transcaucasian state.

On 26 May, Georgia proclaimed itself independent, under German protection. The following day, Azerbaijan did likewise with the connivance of Turkey: this marked the birth of a state whose name indicated a sympathy to Persian Azerbaijan and which contained a mixed population (Tatar, Russian, Persian, Armenian) corresponding to no one national entity. The Tatar element, which gradually became the largest, took some time to forge the notion 'Azerbaijani' or 'Azeri', which changed gradually from meaning 'inhabitant of Azerbaijan' to 'Muslim inhabiting Azerbaijan', thus turning the large and ancient Christian minority into foreigners in the country. The capital of this new state for the moment was Ganja (formerly Elizavetpol) since Baku was in the hands of the Communists, a 'Bolshevik fief', known at that time as the 'Baku Commune' ruled by 26 People's Commissars, including Shahumian. In March 1918, Tatar attempts to destroy this power were defeated with heavy bloodshed and the massacre, by the Armenians, of large numbers of Muslims. Armenia, surrounded by two independent republics, had no choice but to declare its own independence, which it did on 28 May. A few days beforehand, the Armenians had succeeded, in desperate circumstances, in stopping the Turkish advance at the village of Sardarabad.

The victory of Sardarabad became part of Armenian national legend. But their situation remained critical, and the young Republic of Armenia proceeded immediately to negotiate with Ottoman Turkey. It was obliged, by the terms of the Treaty of Batum (4 June) to agree to move back its western frontier considerably, even ceding Alexandropol and most of Nakhichevan to the Ottoman Empire. The frontier between the republics of Armenia and Azerbaijan was then the subject of dispute, in particular with regard to Karabagh and Zangezur. It was there that the Armenian partisan leader, Andranik, concentrated: refusing to acknowledge either the Treaty of Batum, or the republic which had signed it, he counted on the support of the only anti-Turkish elements in the area: the Soviet of Baku and the British forces, which were coming up from Iran. He was soon disillusioned; the first collapsed in September 1918, while the second rapidly adopted a policy favourable to Azerbaijan. Meantime, Andranik concentrated on protecting Zangezur from a possible aggression by the Turks, who would have received the support of the local Tatars; and he turned the region into an Armenian rampart protecting Karabagh on the west.

# 11

## SECURING ARMENIAN KARABAGH: 1918-1920

Mountainous Karabagh, an Armenian stronghold inaccessible to the Tatars, became *de facto* independent, as decreed by the first 'Congress of the Armenians of Karabagh', held at Shushi on 5 August 1918. Representatives of all the villages had appointed a National Council which refused to accept the authority of the Musavat party, and prevented the Turks from subjugating Karabagh in order to continue their advance on Baku and destroy the Bolshevik commune there. The region thus set up what was in fact an independent government, composed of seven persons.[56] Meanwhile the Muslims, continuing their policy of isolating the region, tried to cut off Karabagh from Zangezur. On 26 August 1918, they launched a continuing attack against the Armenian villages lying between the two districts, destroying them one by one. Such was the fate of the large village of Karakeshlagh (or Karakishlak), between Shushi and Goris, which was razed to the ground in September.

In Constantinople, meantime, the delegates of the Republic of Armenia allowed themselves to be duped by Ottoman politicians. Thus, when one of them, Alexander Khatisian, protested to the Minister of the Interior, Talaat, against the Turkish plans for an attack on Karabagh, Talaat telephoned his colleague at the War Ministry, Enver. Reassurances were given to Armenian representative of their 'peaceful intentions' in relation to Karabagh. The Armenians of Karabagh, more realistic, placed their faith in Andranik, whose plans were delayed by an uprising of the Muslims in Zangezur. On 20 September 1918, they convened their second Congress, protesting in vain to the Turkish authorities, and even sending a delegation to the commander of the Second Ottoman division, based at Aghdam, the key town in the east of Karabagh, still held by the Turks. The response was negative. The Turks demanded that they disarm and submit, in order to permit the Turkish forces to march on Shushi.

The situation was examined by the third Congress of the Karabagh Armenians, convened on 1 October. Two days later, the Ottoman com-

mander, Nuri Pasha, arrived at Aghdam and presented a 24-hour ultimatum. Although the population was determined to fight despite having numerically much inferior forces, the Armenian Council sent a delegation to Aghdam to negotiate. But it was to no avail: on 22
September, before the delegation had even reached Aghdam, a Turkish
force of 5000 men, armed with cannon, poured into the Karkar valley.
Their advance on Shushi was retarded by the resistance put up in all
the villages, but they were sacked one by one. On 3 October 1918,
with the aid of the large Muslim population in the lower town,
the Ottoman army entered Shushi. Arrests, plunder and massacres
followed.[57]

But Mountainous Karabagh consisted of more than just its capital,
and the 2000 Turkish troops occupying Shushi were not enough to
control the whole district. The Armenians were aware that, in the
event of defeat, they would meet the same fate as that suffered by their
compatriots in the Ottoman Empire in 1915. The aim of the invaders
was to Turkify the area in order to attach it permanently to Azerbaijan.
This time their plan failed. After launching three unsuccessful attacks
against the town of Martakert, which controls the northern road of
Karabagh, they retreated northwards, wreaking their revenge by committing massacres at Chailu. The Turkish command at Shushi then
turned to the districts of Varanda and Dizak, to the east and south-
east; and on the evening of 31 October, troops accompanied by
heavy artillery set out from the capital with the aim of joining up
with the Tatar reinforcements which had arrived from the eastern
Karabagh plain.

But they had reckoned without the determination of the Armenians
and the remarkable military skill shown by a young man of 30, Aslan
Muradkhanian, in organizing the forces of the villages on both banks
of the river Varanda. The Turks fell into an ambush and, on 2 November, their troops were decimated: only about 80 of them escaped, leaving a large booty behind them. Some days later, an even larger force
was sent out from Shushi to Varanda, but it quickly retreated, finding
all the roads blocked; and soon afterwards, Turkey lost the war and the
Ottoman armies evacuated Mountainous Karabagh.[58]

These two months of September-October 1918 were decisive for
Mountainous Karabagh. The two victories at Martakert and Varanda
saved Armenian Karabagh, threatened with destruction. That the Bolsheviks, who closely followed events in Transcaucasia, were anxious
about the situation is clear from a letter written to Lenin by
Orjonikidze, his close ally, on 12 October: 'In the occupied regions, the
Turks have massacred half the population of Karabagh. They have

invaded the districts of Shushi and Zangezur. The population is putting up strong resistance. Andranik has just been treacherously killed in Karabagh'.[59] This last piece of news was false, but it is an indication of the prestige of the Armenian fighter, even amongst the Bolsheviks.

## Great Britain and Karabagh

A new factor appeared in the autumn of 1918. This was Great Britain, whose diplomacy was to prove damaging for the Armenians. Turkish designs on Baku, with its strategic oil, together with the formation of the Turko-Tatar 'army of Islam', disquieted the British who, early in 1918, despatched an army under the command of General L.C. Dunsterville from Baghdad to northern Iran.[60] In the course of the operation the aim of the British forces in Transcaucasia gradually changed: having come, originally, for the purpose of halting the Turkish advance, they gradually concentrated on countering the Bolshevik threat, against which Denikin's White Army was fighting in the north of the region. Against the advice of Shahumian, the Soviet of Baku, in the face of the Turkish threat, invited the British to enter the town; but in mid-September, when the situation there worsened, the British made haste to leave. The capture of Baku by the Turks a month later was followed by a gruesome, although predictable, massacre of thousands of Armenians; Shahumian and the Commissars were executed with the possible connivance of the British, and Baku became the new capital of the Republic of Azerbaijan.

The autumn of 1918 also marked the end of World War I, and the defeat of the Central Powers, including the Ottoman Empire, which signed the armistice of Mudros on 30 October. In accordance with the conventions between the Allies – more or less tacit – the British were left in charge of the Caucasus. Their policy was inspired by two aims, sometimes contradictory, but both anti-Bolshevik: to support Denikin's White Army forces in the north, and in the south to favour a strong and pro-British Azerbaijan. Many British officers, having served in India, were pro-Muslim. They disliked native Christians. And it must be remembered that the British Empire, thanks to its numerous colonies in Africa and Asia, was a great power in the Muslim world, even perhaps a great Muslim power. General Thomson entered Baku on 17 November; he quickly disappointed the Armenians, whose hopes had been raised by the signing of the armistice.

The British command, with a force of 30,000 soldiers in Transcaucasia, began by calling on the Karabagh Armenians, after the evacuation of the Ottoman armies, to submit to the Azeri authorities, which they refused to do. Armenian Karabagh was awaiting the hero of Zangezur, whose arrival had been announced. In October already, the local military authorities of Karabagh had appealed to Andranik, but he wanted confirmation that he should arrive. There was also the fact that not all the leaders were in favour of calling on Andranik, preferring to await the outcome of negotiations with the Muslims, who were blocking the road between the two regions. Valuable time was thus lost, and it was not until the end of November that Andranik set out. It took him three days to force his way through, after serious fighting.

On 2 December he finally entered the province but, before reaching Shushi, he received, in the village of Avdallar, a message from General Thomson warning him not to go any further. He stopped and soon received an 'explanatory' letter: Germany had also capitulated, and therefore military operations were to be suspended pending the results of the Paris Peace Conference, which was to settle all issues, including those affecting Armenia. Andranik's return to Goris filled the Armenian population of Karabagh with consternation, and encouraged the Tatars, who proceeded to attack the Armenian villages in the south, demolishing the last Christian strongholds between Karabagh and Zangezur. Thus as a result of the warning of a British general, this historic opportunity to attach Karabagh, once and for all, to the Armenian Republic, was not taken.[61]

British promises, moreover, were merely another enticement: at Baku, the representatives of London negotiated with the Musavatists for the attachment to Azerbaijan of Zangezur and Mountainous Karabagh, and this was the decision that the British in December submitted to Shushi, pending the decisions of the Paris Peace Conference.[62] Neither the protests of the Armenians of Karabagh, who refused to obey, nor those of the Armenian government, had any effect. On the contrary, British diplomacy proceeded to take a third anti-Armenian measure: it supported the appointment on 15 January, by Baku, of Khosrov bek Sultanov as governor-general of Karabagh and the surrounding districts, including Zangezur.

This rich landowner, a leading member of the Musavat party, pan-Turkist and anti-Armenian, had played a part in the massacre of Armenians at the time of the liquidation of the Baku Commune. Whilst his authority over Zangezur, which the Armenians had controlled since the time of Andranik, continued to be purely theoretical, the position was different in Shushi, where he assumed his functions on 10 February 1919, having decided to settle the problem of Karabagh – where power was still in the hands of the Armenian National Council – 'once and for all'. The objections raised by the Armenian government in Yerevan had no effect on the British plans. Faced with this situation, the Fourth Congress of the Karabagh Armenians, meeting in Shushi on 12 February, persisted in its refusal to submit to Baku and protested against the appointment of Sultanov: 'Karabagh has never recognized the authority of the Azerbaijani government inside its frontiers, nor will it ever do so'.[63]

Faced with the negative attitude taken by the authorities since the beginning of the year, the Karabagh Armenians again appealed to Andranik, who had followed events from Goris in the neighbouring district of Zangezur, and refused to obey British orders to hand over the district to the Baku authorities. The presence of Andranik in the neighbourhood constituted a threat to the plans of Sultanov, who was supported by the British and the Musavatists. In the spring of 1919, these 'allies' dispatched delegations to Andranik in Goris. Many of his close companions had already left the province. On bad terms with the Dashnak authorities in Yerevan, furious with the attitude of the British, Andranik, who was more of a warrior than a diplomat, decided to leave. The only person he still respected was the Catholicos. In order to go to Echmiadzin, the British proposed that he should go to Tiflis by the Shushi-Evlakh road, and from there to Shamkhor, through the heart of Tatar territory. Fearing that this route would prove a trap, Andranik was persuaded against taking it by the Armenians of Karabagh. On 2 April, he set off for Echmiadzin via the Armenian mountains, after handing over the province of Zangezur to the Yerevan authorities. Its defence against the Turks was soon to be led by another famous Armenian partisan, Nzhdeh.[64]

Meantime, Karabagh continued the struggle. A delegation convened on 26 March 1919 heard from the lips of Colonel D.I. Shuttleworth, who was later to replace Thomson, the following threat: 'We are strong enough to force you to submit'.[65] The mayor of Shushi again replied that the town would never accept Azeri domination. This was confirmed by the Fifth Congress of the Karabagh Armenians, meeting at Shushi on 23 April 1919, where Shuttleworth himself called on the National Armenian Council to submit to Baku. They refused: 'Azerbaijan is and has always been an ally of the Turks, and has taken part in all the atrocities committed by the Turks against the Armenians, and in particular the Armenians of Karabagh'.[66]

With British support, renewed by Shuttleworth on 3 April, Sultanov then decided to apply strong measures: terror and famine. On 20 May, he cut off all roads leading to the Karabagh plain. All trading with the Armenians was forbidden on pain of death. The blockade gradually brought famine to Mountainous Karabagh; and at the same time Sultanov, imitating the methods of the 'Red Ottoman Sultan', Abdul Hamid, organized terrorist brigades of Kurdish irregulars, two of them led by his brothers. As a result, further Armenian villages were destroyed. Khaibalikend is a symbol of Anglo-Tatar connivance. On the same day, 500 corpses were discovered in Shushi; other villages – Kerkjan, Pahlou and others – suffered the same fate. On 12 June, British representatives left Karabagh, leaving Sultanov to continue without restraint. The strong protests made at Echmiadzin by the church, and at Yerevan and Tiflis, had no effect. Sultanov increased the repression. The Armenian leaders were either sent into exile or arrested on orders from Sultanov. Many of them had already gone underground.

In view of the gravity of the situation, the Sixth Congress of Karabagh Armenians met on 28 June at Shosh, west of Shushi. There were vigorous discussions, and the principle of coming to a provisional agreement with the Musavat authorities was agreed on. A delegation of three Armenians was sent to Baku, with powers to negotiate. One of them was killed on the way, and the two others returned to submit the terms of the agreement. They were accompanied by Sultanov himself, who stayed in the Armenian quarter of Shushi, and was extremely affable with the Armenians, even going so far as to re-open the Shushi-Evlakh road: another ruse, to conceal military preparations. Meantime, there was growing dissension amongst the Armenians: the village people, opposed to any kind of submission to the Azeris, regarded the town-dwellers, who were more in favour of an agreement, with mistrust.

It was on 12 August, again at Shosh, that the Seventh Congress opened. With a view to breaking the resistance of the hard-liners, Sultanov appeared on the 14 August, with an ultimatum to the effect that the Baku negotiations must be undertaken within 48 hours. He submitted carefully prepared 'military arguments' in support of this demand, and succeeded in convincing the majority of the Armenians. On 15 August the Congress recognized, 'provisionally', ie. pending the conclusions of the Paris Conference, the authority of the Azerbaijani government; while preserving its own governing bodies, in particular the Armenian Council. The agreement was signed on 22 August.[67] It was a victory for Sultanov, although it failed to satisfy him, owing to the continued existence of the Armenian governing bodies. It also marked the zenith of a shady British policy. Having sown the seeds of future conflicts, the British withdrew from Karabagh at the end of 1919 and later from the whole of Caucasia.

The policy of Great Britain in Karabagh, more or less openly allied with the Musavats of Azerbaijan, was contemporary with the new French policy adopted in Cilicia, of closer relations with the Kemalist Turks. In both cases, the 'allies' were contributing to drive the Armenians out of the area. This aim was achieved in Cilicia but not in Karabagh where, despite the lack of any outside aid, the population resisted all attempts to drive them out.

But it is no exaggeration to say that the present (1991) problem of Karabagh is due largely to British diplomacy in the first half of the year 1919, the effect of which was to prevent Mountainous Karabagh from being permanently attached to Armenia. Thus Colonel J.C. Plowden, the British military representative in Yerevan, declared at the end of August 1919: 'The handing over of Karabagh to Azerbaijan was I think the bitterest blow of all... being the cradle of their race and their last traditional sanctuary, their last refuge when their country has been invaded. It is Armenian in every particular way and the strongest part of Armenia, both financially, militarily and socially.'[68]

## The destruction of Shushi

Owing to the many problems with which it was grappling at the time, the Republic of Armenia was unable to do much to help its compatriots in Karabagh. The Ottoman capitulation had given it an unhoped for opportunity to enlarge its territory, reduced at the time to the region of Yerevan and Lake Sevan. At the end of December 1918, Dro, another famous Armenian military leader, recovered the town of Alexandropol (later Leninakan, now Kumairi) in the north-west, and then advanced against the Georgians in the northern part of Lori. The district of Kars had been given by the Treaty of Brest-Litovsk to the Ottoman Empire, and Nakhichevan was claimed by Azerbaijan; with regard to these two districts the British refrained from opposing the Republic of Armenia, which was thus able to add them to its territory in the spring of 1919. But all was not straightforward. The Allies had still not recognized the Transcaucasian republics and the Paris Peace Conference was in no hurry to settle these territorial problems; and moreover, Armenia was up against the problems of the large Turco-Tartar populations in these disputed regions, which did not recognize Yerevan's authority.

In Karabagh, the end of 1919 brought further difficulties. At the end of November, an agreement was signed between the Armenians and Sultanov, under the aegis of the American Colonel W.H. Haskell, representing the Allied High Commission. But it was meaningless. Haskell proved to be a crook, selling to Azerbaijan the aid which had been sent for Armenia from Europe and America and acting so as to encourage Baku's designs on Karabagh. At the beginning of 1920, Sultanov renewed his threats, first verbally at Shushi, and then in a letter to the Armenian National Council, in which he threatened to raze Karabagh to the ground.[69] A peace delegation sent by the Council to Baku, on 20 February, was sent back to Shushi by the Musavatists.

Meanwhile, the international situation was changing radically. The collapse of Denikin's Volunteer Army naturally reinforced the position of Soviet Russia and its Red Army, then on the borders of Transcaucasia. In addition, an alliance between the two major forces in the region – Bolshevism in Russia and Kemalism in Turkey – was gradually taking shape. The Allies realized, belatedly, that they needed the buffer formed by the Transcaucasian republics, which were at last *de facto* recognized in January 1920. This recognition, however, brought Armenia no positive results. The new geo-political situation was to lead to the collapse of the Musavatist government in Azerbaijan.

Before its demise, this government was to leave a terrible legacy: the destruction of Armenian Shushi. Sultanov had prepared the way by providing the Muslim population with large quantities of arms and sending to Karabagh large reinforcements of Azeri troops. In his thinking the term 'provisional' was to be deleted from the 22 August agreement. He first ringed Karabagh with troops and then, on 19 February 1920, called on the Armenian Council to agree, unconditionally, to the integration of Karabagh in Azerbaijan. At the Eighth Congress, meeting on 28 February in order to give its reply, the division into two factions was clear; there were in effect two distinct assemblies. At Shushi, the minority (mostly Bolsheviks and town-dwellers) was ready to compromise. Meantime, at Shosh the majority, including the Dashnaks, took a harder line, categorically refusing integration in Azerbaijan. They denounced the attitude of Sultanov, the violations of the agreement, in particular the military reinforcement – and also the constant crimes: 'Never had the Armenian population witnessed so many crimes, murders and economic offenses as after the signing of the agreement'.[70] Sultanov, thereupon, stepped up his military preparations. By the beginning of March, it was clear that an attack on Armenian Karabagh was imminent. The Turkish generals Nuri Pasha and Khalil Pasha, former Ittihadists who had transferred their allegiance to Kemalism, arrived to support the attack.

Faced with this situation, the Armenians decided to move first, and organized a rising on the night of 22-23 March, the date of the Muslim New Year. After several days of violent fighting, the Azeri army, on 4

April, entered Shushi. The town was ransacked, thousands of houses were burnt down and the majority of the inhabitants massacred. Sultanov had Rubeni, the founder of the Communist Party of Karabagh, beheaded, after which his head, carried on a spike, was paraded throughout the region.[71] Bishop Vartan and other dignitaries were to meet the same fate. One of the principal members of the Armenian government, Simon Vratsian, was later to admit: 'Events showed that the organizers of the rising lacked experience. The consequences would have been even worse but for the arrival, on 13 April, of Dro and his troops'.

### Azerbaijan sovietized

The Turkification of Shushi was the epitaph of the Musavat. Profiting from the fact that the bulk of the Azeri army was operational in Karabagh, the 11th Red Army entered Baku on 27 April, and the next day, without any real fighting, Azerbaijan became the first Soviet Republic in Transcaucasia. As to the Republic of Armenia and the problem of Karabagh, the Bolshevik Azeri leaders pursued the policy of their predecessors, basing their claims on the affirmation – which was false – that these regions had formerly been under the authority of the Musavat. Some of the Russian Bolsheviks took a more objective view of the problem: B.V. Legrand, G.K. Orjonikidze and, in particular, G.V. Chicherin, the Commissar for Foreign Affairs, who proposed that these territories 'should be occupied not by Azerbaijani but by Russian troops until a favourable political climate was established'.[72] (Armenia itself was not to be Sovietized until the end of 1920.) They were opposed by other Bolsheviks, such as Stalin who agreed with the policy of Nariman Narimanov, Sultanov's emulator, who had become the strong man of Soviet Azerbaijan.

In Karabagh, meantime, Dro was striving to form another army, recruiting from the two southern districts, Varanda and Dizak, the only ones he controlled for the moment. It was there, in the village of Taghavard, on 23 April, that the Ninth Congress of the Karabagh Armenians decided to unite with Armenia. This revolt of Karabagh, supported by Yerevan via Zangezur, furnished yet another opportunity for the attachment of Karabagh to Armenia. But several days later, after the Sovietization of Azerbaijan, the Baku authorities called on the Republic of Armenia to evacuate both Zangezur and Karabagh: they had little to fear from the Bolsheviks at that time, when Azerbaijan was already Sovietized and Armenia still in the hands of the Dashnaks. Under pressure from the 11th Red Army, and weakened by a Communist revolt which had broken out in May 1920, the Armenian government gave in, and ordered Dro to evacuate Karabagh. It was, therefore, a case of the tacit acceptance of the Sovietization of Karabagh, confirmed by the entry of the 11th Red Army at the end of the month; after which it awaited the opportunity to go on to Zangezur, which was defended by General Nzhdeh.

Current with these events, there was an Armenian delegation in Moscow, the 'Levon Shant Mission,' for the purpose of normalizing relations between Moscow and Yerevan, and protecting Armenia from Turkey, where Kemalism was increasing in strength and claiming the Brest-Litovsk frontiers, including the district of Kars. On the question of the three disputed territories, Chicherin proposed that Zangezur and Nakhichevan be given to Armenia, and that a referendum be held on the subject of Mountainous Karabagh. At the end of June there was a second proposal, much less radical: Nakhichevan to go to Armenia, Karabagh to Azerbaijan, and the status of Zangezur to be decided by Legrand, as special Soviet envoy. Armenia delayed its reply, still trusting in the deliberations of the Paris Peace Conference, and then made a curious proposal, asking not only for Mountainous Karabagh but also for Lowland Karabagh, the plain inhabited by Tatars whose status had never, until then, been questioned.

Once again, both in Paris and also in Yerevan and Moscow, Armenian policy faltered, whilst at the same time, in Moscow, shrewd Turkish diplomats were proposing the reinforcement of Kemalo-Bolshevik links, full of future promise. Meanwhile in Soviet Azerbaijan, the government was doing all in its power to annex the three disputed regions; but its arguments failed to convince the Bolshevik leaders. When Lenin, on 22 June, asked him 'whether it was not possible to reach agreement with Narimanov', Chicherin replied 'Karabagh is an authentically Armenian territory'.[73] Moscow had no fixed views on the subject. Thus Chicherin, while he was presenting, his views to the Shant mission, wrote on 19 June 1920 to Orjonikidze that these territories 'should not be attached either to Armenia or to Azerbaijan, but should be placed under the authority of the Russian occupation forces and should set up local Soviets'.[74] In short, he sought occupation by Russian troops rather than attachment to Soviet Azerbaijan whose leader, Narimanov, was accused by Chicherin of 'connivance with Muslim factions'.[75]

This policy was put into practice as from the beginning of July 1920. The 11th Red Army, already firmly installed in Karabagh, came into military conflict, in Zangezur, with the Armenian army led by Dro. But neither re-attachment to Yerevan nor occupation by the Red Army satisfied Narimanov, who openly criticized Chicherin, and changed his tactics. He stated that it was essential 'to incite the populations of the regions in question to pronounce in favour of union with Azerbaijan'.[76] The methods proposed were explained in the secret correspondence addressed to his counterparts in Zangezur by Asad Karaiev, the president of the Karabagh revolutionary committee and one of the Bolshevik authorities of Azerbaijan, close to Narimanov. On 19 July 1920 Karaiev wrote: 'We know that our troops were defeated and had to retreat; but now, instead of the army, our money is doing miracles... The government has decided to pay 200 million roubles for the attachment of Karabagh and Zangezur to Azerbaijan'. Two days later, Karaiev expressed himself in even more explicit terms in a letter (quoted in full as DOCUMENT 2). Its postscript would not have been disavowed by Talaat Pasha and the other Turkish leaders responsible for the genocide of 1915.[77]

## DOCUMENT 2

### - TOP SECRET – SHUSHI, 21 JULY 1920

**The provincial revolutionary committee of Karabagh to the regional revolutionary committee at Goris.**

*Comrades who have just arrived say that 90% of the villages of Zangezur have not yet been disarmed. This is regrettable, but what is even more regrettable is that the Armenian population of Zangezur has not yet been decapitated [ie. deprived of its leaders]. Its intelligentsia and its military chiefs are still present in the villages. Tomorrow, in the event of a rising, they will assume the leadership and drive our forces out of Zangezur. I repeat this again and again: no time must be lost. You must work night and day. See to it that all the important Armenian personalities are arrested. Deportations and pillaging are of little importance.*

*Time will pass, the situation will change, and they will return to their country. Leave aside all humane considerations. It is not with such sentiment that one builds a state, conquers countries or lives in peace. Our comrades here are not content with the members of the Armenian revolutionary committee of Gerusi [Goris]. Try to arrange for new elections to be held, and to allow on to the committee only Muslims and Rus-*

*sians we know. Armenak Karagueuzian should soon be arriving in Gerusi. He is late because he has not received his money. Until he has obtained 22 million roubles, he will not leave.*

*Now is the time to get rich, so why not take the opportunity to do so? So let him profit from the money that our government is giving him! He promises to have Zangezur attached to Azerbaijan in seven days. We are sure that you will very soon give us the good news of the attachment of Ghapan. If you have not sufficient forces, use money instead. Why do you delay the attachment of this rebel region by talking of the existence of a certain Azhda [Nzhdeh] Pasha? Use the consecrated methods! What Armenian, in return for three million roubles, would not bring us the head of this man? If you need money, send us a telegram and we shall send some.*

Salutations. Asad Karaiev.

*PS. In order to weaken the Armenians in places where the guerilla force is active, you have only to kill a Russian soldier and accuse the Armenians of the crime. You know very well what the Russians will do [to them]. Let not a single honest man exist in Zangezur, and leave no money either, so that this accursed people [the Armenians] will never rise again.*

Asad Karaiev

# 12

# THE END OF THE REPUBLIC
# OF ARMENIA

The solution recommended by Chicherin was adopted the following month. Armenia, not being strong enough to resist the Red Army, had to agree to the Bolshevik occupation of the three disputed regions and, on 10 August 1920, signed an agreement in Tiflis with Legrand, the representative of Soviet Russia: Russia thus occupied Karabagh, Zangezur and Nakhichevan, in order to create favourable conditions for an equitable solution of the territorial disputes between Armenia and Azerbaijan. These 'conditions' probably implied, in the minds of the Bolsheviks, the Sovietization of Armenia, in the immediate future. Ironically, it was the same day, 10 August, that saw the signature of the Treaty of Sèvres, opening up glorious prospects for Armenia – which never materialized, since no outside power was willing to commit troops to the defence of Armenia.[78]

Another irony came from the attitude of the British government. Whereas it had done a great deal to oppose Armenian sovereignty over the regions in question, the Foreign Office now condemned the agreement of 10 August, accusing the Armenians of betraying Britain. The balance of power had now changed. Bolshevism was gaining fast in south Russia and Transcaucasia, as was Kemalism in Anatolia. And the three disputed territories – Karabagh, Zangezur and Nakhichevan – formed the link between these two enemies of Britain, who realized, belatedly, that to back the Armenians might have made more sense.

As was to be expected, the 'provisional' occupation of the disputed regions was followed by measures of bolshevization not provided for in the Tiflis agreement, and against which the Armenian government protested to Legrand in vain. Several Dashnak leaders were executed in Karabagh, and in Zangezur a number of villages were razed to the ground. But it was in western Armenia that the danger was mortal. For several months, Karabekir, the commander of the Kemalist troops on the eastern front, had been waiting impatiently, dreaming of launching an attack on Armenia. Kemal was more diplomatic and was waiting for a favourable opportunity to fulfil his aims: he had to consider the

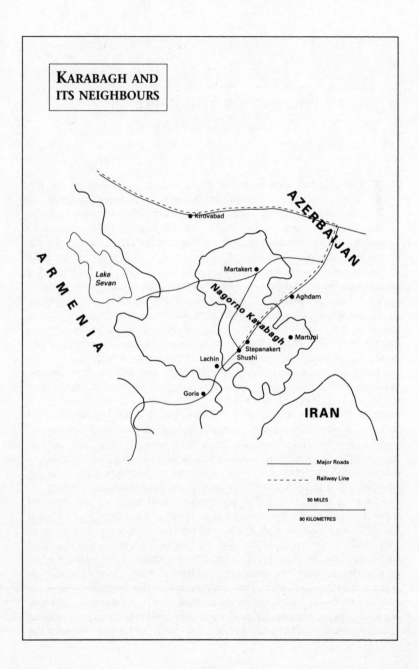

KARABAGH AND
ITS NEIGHBOURS

AZERBAIJAN

● Kirovabad

A R M E N I A

*Lake Sevan*

Martakert ●

Nagorno Karabagh

● Aghdam

● Martuni

Lachin ●   Stepanakert
Shushi

Goris ●

IRAN

———————— Major Roads

– – – – – – Railway Line

50 MILES

80 KILOMETRES

susceptibilities of Soviet Russia, who feared possible Turkish designs on Baku.

The green light was given in September 1920. Soviet Russia, though not in favour of this offensive, had no reason to aid Armenia, 'an ally of the Entente', albeit one with whom no alliance was active. Unfortunately too, Britain advised Armenia against making any agreement with either the Soviets or the Kemalists, at the time when a minimum might still have been saved. It advised Armenia against agreement, but did nothing to assist. Karabekir's offensive was pitiless and devastating. Kars fell on 30 October, Alexandropol on 7 November. Abandoned once again, Armenia signed an armistice on 18 November 1920.

These Turkish successes caused increasing anxiety in Moscow, which decided to keep an 'Armenian buffer' between Turkey and Baku. The price was that Armenia should be sovietized. The Red Army entered Armenia at the end of November 1920; and on 2 December, the Dro-Legrand agreements confirmed the Sovietization of Armenia (including Zangezur). But the frontiers were not yet settled – a question decided on the western front. On the night of 2-3 December 1920, Karabekir, relentless, forced the Dashnaks to sign the Treaty of Alexandropol, which confined Armenia within the frontiers fixed by the Treaty of Batum: it lost the district of Kars, Nakhichevan, and Zangezur, and became, in fact, a Turkish protectorate. Paradoxically, this treaty was signed by the superseded government of Armenia. The actual government had changed meantime, and had become Soviet.[79]

## Sovietized Armenia

The Sovietization of a truncated Armenia opened a new chapter in the history of the three regions, now disputed between two Soviet republics. Already on 9 November, Stalin had said that Zangezur and Karabagh 'cannot be handed back to Dashnak Armenia',[80] but without excluding the possibility that they might be handed over to a future Sovietized Armenia. On 30 November, the very day after the entry of the Red Army into Armenia, Narimanov, president of the revolutionary Committee of Azerbaijan, sent his Armenian counterpart an astonishing telegram, stating explicitly, in a 'burst of enthusiasm': 'As of today, the old frontiers between Armenia and Azerbaijan are declared to be non-existent. Mountainous Karabagh, Zangezur and Nakhichevan are recognized to be integral parts of the Socialist Republic of Armenia'. This apparent about-face on the part of a person who had always taken the opposite view was to prove later to be a tactical device.

The text was published on the following day. The Azerbaijani 'ultras' regarded it as treachery, and called on the Muslims of Nakhichevan to turn to Turkey. The Bolsheviks, on the contrary, were full of praise for this act of 'authentic internationalism'. Orjonikidze described it as 'an historic document unprecedented in the history of humanity'. He informed Lenin and Stalin, on 2 December that 'Azerbaijan had proclaimed already yesterday the attachment of Nakhichevan, Zangezur and Karabagh to Soviet Armenia'.[81] On 4 December 1920, Stalin himself in *Pravda*, confirmed in rapturous terms: 'Soviet Azerbaijan has officially renounced its claim to the disputed territories.... The age-old conflict between Armenia and its Muslim neighbours has been settled in one fell swoop'.[82] But the situation on the spot was far more complex.

Zangezur was to present many problems for the Bolsheviks, whose repressive measures gave rise to revolts at the end of 1920. The strong man in Zangezur was the able Dashnak fighter Nzhdeh, who had been fighting successfully against the Tatars since November 1919. On 25 December 1920, Zangezur proclaimed itself independent. And, after the defeat, on 2 April, of the Dashnak rebels who, on 18 February 1921, had seized power in Yerevan, Zangezur became for several months the last stronghold of anti-Bolshevik resistance. It was there, in effect, that Nzhdeh proclaimed the 'Independent Republic of Mountainous Armenia'. It was crushed in July with the aid of detachments of the Red Army sent from Karabagh. There is little doubt that Zangezur became thenceforth an integral part of Soviet Armenia due to Nzhdeh: following in the footsteps of Andranik, he succeeded in 're-Armenizing' the region, making Baku's claims to it even weaker.

Nakhichevan's fate was to be different, despite Narimanov's promises. The infiltration of the Turkish army stationed in the vicinity gave Ankara certain rights there. The problem was settled, without consulting the Armenians, between the Turks and the Soviets. By the Soviet-Turkish Treaty of Moscow (16 March 1921), ratified by the treaty of Kars (13 October 1921), between Turkey and the three Soviet Transcaucasian republics, Nakhichevan was declared autonomous 'under the protection of Azerbaijan', but it was stipulated that 'this protection could not be transferred to another state'.[83] This constituted a blatant instance of Turkish interference: it was under pressure from Ankara that the decision was taken to transfer a region which was Armenian by both its history and much of its population to a Turkic Soviet Republic with which it was not even geographically connected.

## Karabagh separated from Armenia

After this failure over Zangezur and success over Nakhichevan, the time had come for Narimanov to tackle the 'third piece'. Repudiating his declarations of December 1920, he now claimed Karabagh for Azerbaijan. In this he had the support of Stalin whose position had been defined in a letter to Orjonikidze: 'It is essential to take sides firmly with one of the two parties, in the present case, of course, Azerbaijan, and also Turkey.' This declaration was in complete contradiction to the terms of the agreement signed on 12 May 1921 between the representatives of Soviet Armenia and those of the Red Army which confirmed the Armenian character of Zangezur and Karabagh. The question was examined by the Caucasian Bureau of the Communist Party on 3 June 1921, which decreed, in the presence of Narimanov himself, that Mountainous Karabagh belonged to Armenia. Several days later, the decree of the Armenian government, published both in Yerevan and in Baku, made the position quite clear: 'Mountainous Karabagh henceforth constitutes an integral part of the Soviet Socialist Republic of Armenia'. Narimanov thereupon threatened to permit 'the re-formation of anti-Soviet groups in Azerbaijan'.[84]

The threat of nationalist agitation in Azerbaijan began to concern the Caucasian Bureau, and it was decided, on the 25 June, to send to Karabagh a commission composed of an Armenian Askanaz Mravian, and an Azeri, Asad Karaiev (the author of the letter included as DOCUMENT 2). When the train arrived at Evlakh, Karaiev tried to persuade Mravian to go to Baku in order to settle the problem. Sensing the trap, Mravian refused and, from Karabagh, cabled to Orjonikidze, stressing the urgency of the situation. Orjonikidze sent word to Narimanov, demanding that he follow the 'principle that no Armenian village may be attached to Azerbaijan, just as no Muslim village may be attached to Armenia'.[85] The vast majority of the villages of Mountainous Karabagh were Armenian. Disregarding this, the political Bureau of the Communist Party of Azerbaijan, on 27 June, refused to restore Mountainous Karabagh to Armenia, on the grounds that the economy of the province was more closely linked to Azerbaijan.

The Caucasian Bureau decided thereupon to meet in Tiflis at the beginning of July 1921 in order finally to settle the frontier problems of Transcaucasia. The future of Mountainous Karabagh was decided at two bizarre meetings. On 4 July the Bureau decided, by a majority vote, that the region should be attached to Armenia. Kirov and Orjonikidze voted for, while Narimanov, furious, demanded that the problem be submitted to the Central Committee.

What followed defied logic. The Bureau accepted Narimanov's proposal, but met again on the 5 July and under pressure from Stalin, was forced to accept, without debate, a motion entirely opposed to the one it had adopted the previous day: 'In view of the need to install national peace between Muslims and Armenians, of the economic links between Mountainous and Lower Karabagh, and of their permanent links with Azerbaijan, it is decided to leave Mountainous Karabagh inside the frontiers of Azerbaijan, giving it a large measure of regional autonomy, and having as its centre the town of Shushi, forming part of the autonomous region'.[86]

Thus it took only one day to reverse a unanimous position which had been held for more than year. It was clear that Mountainous Karabagh, with a 94% Armenian population, should have been re-attached to Armenia, despite the fact that the Tatars had succeeded in cutting it off from Armenia, by emptying a narrow strip of land connecting the two, of its Armenian population. There was a precedent in the situation of Nakhichevan which had been attached to Azerbaijan, even though it was cut off from Azerbaijan by Armenian Zangezur. Nor are the economic arguments valid; and even if they were, they could be used against the attaching of Nakhichevan to Azerbaijan, from which it is entirely separated.

What then explains this complete change by the Soviet authorities? One point is that as time passed, the balance of power became increasingly unfavourable to Armenia. Until Georgia was Sovietized (February 1921), until the Dashnak insurrection was quelled (April) and as long as Zangezur maintained its rebellion – until, in fact, Soviet power was firmly established – the Armenians had had to be conciliated. By the summer of 1921 this was no longer necessary. The rebellion had just been crushed, and the desire to punish the Armenians may have had something to do with this new decision. There were other factors: the economic and demographic importance of Azerbaijan; the special, though somewhat weakened, relations between Moscow and Turkey; the threats of Narimanov ('If Armenia claims Karabagh we shall not supply her with oil'[87]), the regrettable attitude of certain Armenian bolsheviks, on the pretext of 'internationalism' and out of hatred of the Dashnaks; and the influence of Stalin. Lenin, who was ill at the time, later spoke of the problems of 'autonomization': 'I think that Stalin's hastiness and excessive administrative zeal were fated';[88] to which might be added the ethnic suspicion expressed by the Georgian, Stalin, who asked Lenin to put an end to the 'imperialist leanings' of the Armenian people.

These attitudes have continued as seen in the sentiments taken from an official pamphlet published in Moscow in 1988, designed to justify the decision of 5 July 1921: 'Narimanov was one of the outstanding figures of Azerbaijan', and, 'Stalin's stand was internationalist, correct and therefore socialist'.[89]

## The Autonomous Region of Mountainous Karabagh

Thus Mountainous Karabagh was attached to Azerbaijan. The text of 5 July had spoken of 'a large degree of regional autonomy'. The Baku authorities attempted to ignore this aspect, the effect of which would be to limit, at least in theory, their sovereignty over the region. Their position was facilitated by a carefully designed administrative sub-division. But the overwhelming majority of the Armenians protested; on 3 July 1922, through the voice of the Regional Committee of the Communist Party of Shushi, they demanded the administrative unity and autonomous status promised. A few months previously, the three republics had been federated to form the Soviet Socialist Federal Republic of Transcaucasia (a union which was to be dissolved in 1936). Unrest continued in Mountainous Karabagh. A report was presented on 15 February to the regional Committee of Transcaucasia, which examined the question in June 1923.

It was not until 7 July 1923 that the Baku authorities published the decree on the formation of the Autonomous Region of Mountainous Karabagh, the frontiers of which were to be designated on 15 August by a joint Commission. Here again, the Armenians were to be bitterly disappointed. On the one hand, as was to be expected, the frontier on the west excluded the 'corridor' formed by Lachin, Kelbaja and Getabek, which had been deliberately emptied of its Armenian population, in order to cut off Mountainous Karabagh from Armenian Zangezur. On the other hand, there were cut off, on, the north, the districts 'of Shamkhor, Khanlar, Dashkesan and Shahumian (formerly Gulistan), where the population was predominantly Armenian (about 90%)', as pointed out in 1963 in a petition submitted by the Armenians to Khrushchev.[90] Thus the region designated as 'Autonomous' was only one part of the Karabagh populated by Armenians, itself only part of Karabagh as a whole, contained in the former Armenian provinces of Artsakh and Utik.

It was a gloomy summer for Armenia. A little earlier, on 24 July 1923, the Allies had accepted the conditions of Turkey and signed the Treaty of Lausanne, in which the name 'Armenia' was not even mentioned: Western Armenia was obliterated, whilst Eastern Armenia was pitilessly mutilated. On 1 August 1923, it was decided to move the cap-

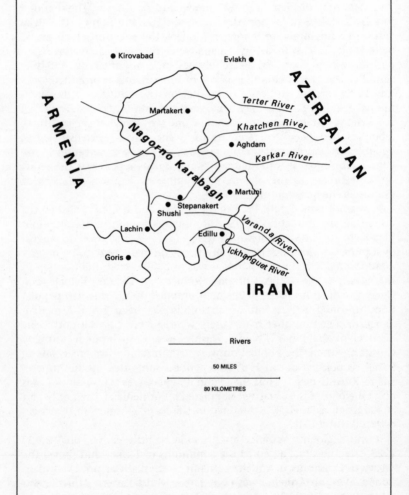

MOUNTAINOUS
KARABAGH

ital of Mountainous Karabagh: Shushi, turkified since March 1920, was replaced as capital by Khankend, 10 kilometres away, renamed on 20 September Stepanakert, after the Bolshevik hero Stepan Shahumian. The first administrative carving up of the autonomous region corresponded, broadly speaking, to four out of the five 'melikdoms'. The districts were thus as follows: Jraberd in the north (with the celebrated monastery of Gandzasar), Khachen in the centre, Varanda in the east (with the ancient monastery of Amaras), Dizak in the south. Khachen was soon divided into two, so as to attach one district (now called Askeran) to Armenian Stepanakert, and the other to Azeri Shushi. The other three districts were, like Shushi, renamed after the respective capitals: Martakert on the north, Martuni on the east, Hadrut to the south. During the first days of November 1923, the first Congress of Soviets of the 'Autonomous Region of Mountainous Karabagh' was opened.

The president of the revolutionary Committee, Karageuzian, was enthusiastic in celebrating the Armenian defeat: 'The Armenian worker-peasant received his autonomy not from imperialism or their Dashnak or Musavat lackeys, but only from the proletariat of Baku and the revolutionary peasantry of neighbouring Azerbaijan'.[91] The evolution of the 'Autonomous Region' from 1923 to 1988 was to give a tragic echo to this derisory statement.

# 13

# THE YEARS OF SUPPRESSION: 1923-1987

## Azeri policy

In all the official Soviet publications, the northern fringe of Azerbaijan (ie. former Atropatene) is shown either as part of the SSR of Azerbaijan or simply as Azerbaijan, with a long and rich past, whereas the region more authentically known as Azerbaijan, south of the Persian frontier, is marked as 'Iranian Azerbaijan'. Roles have been reversed. The Baku historians have attempted to invent an 'Azeri past' by appropriating the Caucasian Albanians, just as the Turks of Ankara appropriated the Hittites in order to forge an Anatolian past. For this purpose, their policy is to refer to this region as the territory of the 'Azeris', ie. of the Muslim population. As late as the 1980s, the official pamphlet on Azerbaijan stated: 'the six million inhabitants of SSR Azerbaijan are not only Azerbaijanis, but also Russians, Armenians, Georgians, Lesghians, Jews...in short representatives of more than 70 nationalities and ethnic groups'.[92] The transition was quickly made: the status of the republic was changed from being multinational to Turkish, and the 10% of Armenians, who had lined there for many centuries, ranked not even as Azerbaijanis, but as part of a multitude of minority peoples.

To complete this picture Baku had to get rid of its two 'autonomous Armenian wounds', ie. Nakhichevan and Karabagh. Nakhichevan, lying between Iran on the south and Soviet Armenia in the north, was raised, on 9 February 1924, to the rank of an 'Autonomous Soviet Socialist Republic' (ASSR) attached to Azerbaijan. In 1917, the Armenian population was 50,000, representing 40% of the total. By 1926, this proportion had dropped to 20% and in 1979, the Armenian population was 3400 or 1.4%.[93] By 1987, on the eve of the Karabagh movement, there remained in Nakhichevan only two Armenian villages, as against 44 in 1917. The Armenian monuments, once so numerous in this cradle of the Armenian people, suffered the same fate. Ankara made no secret of its plans, arranging in January 1932 an exchange of territory with Iran so as to have 10 kilometres of common frontier with Nakhichevan, which was now populated mainly by Turko-Azeris.

The fear of being 'Nakhichevanized' now haunted the autonomous region of Mountainous Karabagh, whose population in 1926 was 125,000, of which 89% were Armenians. This region has become an enclave since the 'clearance' of the valley of the Hagaru river, in order to separate Karabagh from Zangezur, creating a narrow strip of land emptied of Armenians, stretching from Mount Hinal in the north to the banks of the river Araxes. In the middle of this strip lies the town of Lachin, cutting the Goris-Stepanakert road.

## Red Kurdistan

This 'Lachin strip', which was cleared of Armenians before the process of Sovietization, was populated mainly not by Turks but by Kurds, who for a brief period in the 1920s enjoyed autonomy. This fact was recalled in a letter addressed by the Soviet Kurdish intellectuals to the USSR authorities at the beginning of 1988 asking, as Karabagh had, that the Lachin strip should be attached to Armenia. 'In 1923 there was created, in Azerbaijan, the district of Kurdistan, having Lachin as its capital. This district contained Kelbajar, Kubatla, Kurdaji, Murad-khanli and Kara Keshlagh [Kara Kishlak], territories populated by Muslim Kurds.... A technical training school and other cultural centres were opened at Shusha.... But this did not last long ... In 1929, the district of Kurdistan was abolished; subsequently, most of the Kurds were forcibly deported to Kazakhstan and Turkmenia.... After the death of Stalin, in 1957, the garrisons were abolished, and the Kurds were authorized to return to their native land; but it was not possible to revive the life of the district.... Pan-Turkism, stirred up during the Stalin epoch, worked in secret, disguised under the banner of Marxism-Leninism.'

The Kurds were much better treated in Armenia than in Azerbaijan, so they demanded 'that the territory lying between Mountainous Karabagh and Armenia – what had formerly been the district of Kurdistan – be incorporated in the Armenian SSR,... in order to save it from the cultural genocide ordered by the Azeris in 1929 and still being carried out'.[94] It is not quite clear how this 'Red Kurdistan' disappeared, at the time when, on the other side of the frontier, Republican Turkey was engaging in large-scale campaigns against the Kurds.

114

**Exodus of the Karabagh Armenians**

As a result of continuous fighting, the population of Mountainous Karabagh decreased between 1913 and 1923. Between 1923 and the Khrushchev era (1953-1964) information on the population was fragmentary and imprecise because of Stalinism. The Armenian population of the town of Shushi, formerly the third largest town of Transcaucasia, was very much reduced by the massacres of March 1920. From 40,000 inhabitants at the beginning of the 20th century, by 1929 its population had shrunk to only 5000.[95] It was now a Turkish town in an Armenian region, with Lachin to the west and Aghdam on the east, forming a trio of anti-Armenian bastions controlling Mountainous Karabagh. The new capital, the Armenian town of Stepanakert, is situated 10 kilometres to the north in the Karkar valley, and its architecture, like that of Yerevan, was the work of Alexander Tamanian. Its population, only 3000 in 1929, in 1991 reached over 60,000.[96]

It is instructive to compare the official report on the 'cultural and economic development' of Armenian Karabagh under the Soviet regime between 1923 and 1988, with the calamitous picture of the same period drawn, often by the same authors, after the beginning of the 'Karabagh movement', at the end of 1987. On the plus side, there was the opening, in 1924, at Stepanakert, of the Maxim Gorky library, which now possesses 60,000 volumes in three languages (Armenian, Russian, Turkish). In 1932, the Maxim Gorky National Theatre was established. Later, in 1945, the Azerbaijan Academy of Sciences opened a branch at Stepanakert, specializing in agricultural research. The Armenian-language newspaper 'The Peasant of Karabagh' in Armenian founded at Shushi in June 1923, shortly after changed its name to 'Soviet Karabagh' and was published at Stepanakert; it became a daily in 1967. Every district had its Armenian-language daily newspaper, with the exception of *Shusha* (in Azeri Turkish). In 1934 there appeared 'The Young Bolsheviks' a weekly paper which lasted until 1941; also 'The Attack', a monthly, which lasted for only the first number. Another monthly, 'The Spark', which appeared in 1929, published five numbers.[97]

On the minus side, the best proof of the inadequacy of these measures was the decrease of the Armenian population. Their exodus was more or less compensated for, until World War II, by a large natural population growth. But the war caused a serious drain, with 45,000 men called up, and half that number killed. The process of 'de-Armenization' was then accentuated, the exodus of Armenians being parallel to the migration of Turks to Karabagh. Between 1923 and 1987, dozens of Armenian towns and villages disappeared. The figures for the percentage of Armenians in the population can be seen in the following statistics[98]:

| | |
|---|---|
| 1921 | 94.4% |
| 1926 | 89.1% |
| 1939 | 88.1% |
| 1959 | 84.4% |
| 1970 | 80.6% |
| 1979 | 75.9% |

The 1979 census gives approximately 120,000 Armenians out of a population of 160,000. Since 1970, the Azeri-Turkish population has increased by 36.3%, the Armenian by 1.7%. The corresponding figures from 1926 onward are 200% and 10.2%. During the same period, Armenian Zangezur, though much poorer, had its population increased by 120%. In 1979, only one Armenian out of every 10 born in Mountainous Karabagh stayed there and since 1926 an average of 2000 Armenians per year have left. This exodus is of course not a matter of chance, but is due to the persistent policy of Baku, whose aim is to 'Nakhichevanize' the territory, to de-Armenize it, first culturally and then physically.

The Armenian-language schools are attached to the Azeri Ministry of Education, where none of the staff speak Armenian. The schools do not teach the history of Armenia, nor do they receive books from Armenia. Television programmes are in either Turkish or Russian; it was only after the demonstrations of 1988 that Mountainous Karabagh was able to receive Armenian television programmes. These are but a few examples of the methods used to hamper Armenian cultural development.

Special attention was paid to Armenian monuments, the number and artistic quality of which provide the most eloquent proof of the Armenian character of Karabagh. Azeri historians strive in vain to 'prove' that these monuments are not Armenian at all, but Caucasian Albanian, 'and therefore Azeri', and they are left to rot away, or indeed are actually destroyed. Such is the case, in particular, of many *khachkars*, or cross-stones so typical of Armenian art. Needless to say these architectural treasures are systematically ignored in tourist guides to Azerbaijan, which mention only Islamic or revolutionary monuments. Up to a point, due both to inertia and also to the desire 'not to create problems', Armenia connived in this neglect of its monuments. Sites of special significance for modern Armenian history are also being destroyed; the ruins of Khaibalikend, where 600 Armenians were massacred in June 1919, are being demolished, including the church, which was being used as a stable.

It was not until 1980 that there appeared a booklet in Armenian on the monuments of Karabagh which, as only 1500 copies of it were printed, soon became impossible to find. A sign of change: the author, Shahen Mekerchian, was able, in 1985, to publish a second much fuller edition of his book, with a print-run of 10,000 copies, to be followed, in 1988, by a Russian edition of 25,000 copies, with more elaborate illustrations.

These factors largely explain the birth in 1987 of the 'Karabagh movement'. It is important to note that Armenians did not leave Karabagh because of poverty even though Karabagh today gives the impression of underdevelopment, due to a deliberate policy of pauperization, which is periodically condemned. But its land is rich and its fertility contrasts with the rocky, arid soil of Armenia, where only the plain of Ararat can feed a population. Thus both culturally and economically Armenia and Karabagh are mutually complementary.

**The first attempts at re-unification**

Already in the 1920s, an organization, 'Karabagh for Armenia' was set up, having branches as far afield as Gandzak (now Kirovabad). It was, of course, clandestine, and it was composed of ex-members of several political parties. At the beginning of 1927, seven Armenians from Karabagh fled to Iran. From Enzeli, on the Caspian Sea, one of them sent a revealing letter to *Haratch*, the Armenian daily newspaper published in Paris. He spoke of the 'hard times' his compatriots were going through, at the hands both of the Bolsheviks and of the Turkish authorities: 'The Armenian people in Karabagh cannot get used to the idea of being ruled by Azeri Turks.' He also criticized the Bolshevik Armenian leadership in Stepanakert, in the pay of Baku and out of touch with the local population. The organization succeeded, in November 1926, in distributing tracts throughout the whole of Karabagh. This led to numerous arrests, mainly in Communist circles. A second tract was circulated at the end of the month. Its text still has relevance today. 'If the present leaders of Armenia have abandoned the hundreds of thousands of Armenians in Karabagh.... of what use are they, what are they doing living like flunkeys on the banks of the Hrazdan [river; in Armenia]?' It ends with an appeal for the unity of all those who, whether natives of Karabagh or not, are in favour of its re-unification to Armenia.[99]

The organization was liquidated in 1927. Soon afterwards, in 1929, there were again pan-Turkish movements in Azerbaijan, leading to further demands for the re-attachment of Karabagh to Armenia. In 1936, the new Soviet Constitution dissolved the Federation of Transcaucasia, and separated the three republics, without changing their frontiers. The result was to make Karabagh even more dependent on Baku. In Armenia, the timid nationalist leanings of the First Secretary of the Party, Aghasi Khanjian, also affected his attitude to the problem of Karabagh. This was possibly one of the reasons for his assassination in July 1936, on orders from Beria. His successor, Harutunian (also known as Arutunov), made two fruitless approaches to Moscow, in 1945 and in 1949.[100]

## Karabagh in the post-Stalin period

The years of Stalinist terrorism were followed by the Khrushchev 'thaw'.[101] In 1960, on the occasion of the 40th anniversary of the Sovietization of Armenia, people dreamed, in vain, that injustice would be repaired. The circumstances were particularly propitious because the new First Secretary in Yerevan, Zarobian, tended to support the Armenian claims. But he did not survive the fall of Khrushchev. It was in 1963 that the problem was solemnly brought to open notice; on 19 May, a petition signed by 2500 Karabagh Armenians was submitted to Khrushchev. This lengthy text denounced in detail the 'chauvinist policy' of Azerbaijan, designed to 'ruin the economy of the Armenian population and, eventually, to force the Armenians to leave'. One of the methods used was 'to make the institutions and enterprises of Mountainous Karabagh dependent on enterprises in places 40 to 60 kilometres away', such as Aghdam or Barda, outside the Autonomous Region. Moreover, 'in 40 years, not a single kilometre of road has been built to link the villages to the regional centre', and 'nothing had been done to develop agriculture in the region', in addition to which 'culture and education are on the decline'. The situation in the northern Armenian districts not included in the Autonomous Region, was even worse. The petition ended with a demand that Karabagh be attached either to Armenia or to the Russian Federation. Khrushchev turned a deaf ear to this appeal, and the Azeris responded by assassinating 18 Armenians in Karabagh.

After this petition, there were many other demands put forward. On 24 April 1965, the 50th anniversary of the genocide of the Armenians in Turkey, there was a spectacular demonstration in Yerevan, accompanied by spontaneous cries of 'our land' referring both to the Armenian regions in Turkey and to those in Azerbaijan. For Moscow, it was easier to 'satisfy' the first demand (for instance by the erection of a monument) than the second, since the transfer of territories was a matter of internal policy.

In June of that same year of 1965 another petition, addressed to the Communist Party and the government, was sent to Moscow. This petition, asking for Mountainous Karabagh to be re-attached to Armenia, was signed by 13 prominent figures of Karabagh, including Bagrat Ulubabian, who had been, since 1949, president of the Writers' Union of Karabagh. They were, at the end of the year, to be threatened with sanctions. One of the authors of this petition was a young deputy, Arkadi Manucharov, who was later forced to seek exile in Armenia. Returning to Karabagh in 1977, he was to direct the 'Krunk Committee', linked with the 'Karabagh Committee', and was also to be arrested in December 1988. (*Krunk* is Armenian for 'crane', and refers to a well-known poem and song about the bird flying from the homeland.) This 'letter of the 13' obtained 45,000 signatures in Karabagh. This was also the period in which the 'Party of National Unity', which sought for independence in Armenia, but was also deeply concerned with the problems of Nakhichevan and Karabagh was established in Yerevan.

In 1966 it was the turn of Yerevan to send a petition to Moscow demanding the re-attachment of Karabagh to Armenia, but without results. Meantime, the position in Karabagh steadily worsened, since the Azeris were determined to repay the Armenians for their timid protests during the past few years. The request addressed by the Karabagh Armenians to the Yerevan authorities, this time, spoke of cases of illegal imprisonment, murders committed with impunity and official threats. 'Our situation is worse than it ever was, even under the tyrannical reign of the Khans and Musavats... Our honour is besmirched, our dignity and our rights flouted'. At this time, many Armenian intellectuals of Karabagh were forced to go into exile on pain of death. The town of Stepanakert was, in 1968, the scene of clashes between Armenians and Azeris.

Following this, there were several years during which little information filtered through; although it was clear from the clandestine press and other unofficial sources that the situation of the Karabagh Armenians was worsening. Unrest continued, while Mountainous Karabagh was still governed by a leadership appointed by and working in the interests of Baku. This group was exemplified by Boris Kevorkov, the sole Armenian member of the Central Committee of the Azeri Communist Party. He was appointed, in 1973, First Secretary of the Regional Committee for Mountainous Karabagh of the Azerbaijani Communist Party, and, at the head of the Autonomous Region, acted for 15 years as the perfect collaborationist. His hard-line attitude immediately caused 58 prominent Armenians to complain to Moscow – but with no results. The long speech he made, on 21 March 1975, to the plenary session of the Regional Committee is a model of obscurantism. The whole of the intelligentsia of Mountainous Karabagh was accused – writers, poets, journalists (including the editor of 'Soviet Karabagh') and historians (including Ulubabian who was described, with several others, as a 'retrograde nationalist'). Shahen Mekerchian, studying the Armenian monuments of Karabagh, had his work called 'nationalist vanity'. Kevorkov went so far as to order the destruction of a monument to the victims of World War II, on the pretext that the eagle it depicted was an Armenian 'nationalist symbol'.

These attitudes were shared by many of the Armenian economic and political authorities of Mountainous Karabagh. Thus, it is not surprising that the plenary session of the regional committee, held in 1975, though in large majority Armenian, should have rejected the idea of attaching Karabagh to Armenia, describing it as 'Dashnak propaganda'. Arrests and deportations followed.[102] An article in the well-known Soviet journal 'Problems of Peace and Socialism', published in 1977 contained similar ideas. This situation was denounced by the popular writer Sero Khanzadian, a native of Zangezur, who, in a celebrated letter addressed to Brezhnev on 15 October 1977, attacked the leaders of Karabagh, the slanderous letters in the Soviet press and the lying statements of the officials. He concluded by stating that the only solution was to re-unify Karabagh with Armenia. A similar appeal was made in a long series of articles published at the beginning of 1979 in the journal *Baikar* of Boston, Massachusetts, USA, signed enigmatically 'Kevorkian', obviously a pseudonym for a Soviet Armenian historian.

## The perestroika era

After the two decades generally known as the 'Brezhnev stagnation' (1964-1982), the coming to power of Mikhail Gorbachev in 1985 naturally encouraged hopes of re-attaching Karabagh to Armenia, just as had the arrival of Khrushchev after the Stalin terror. The ideas of *perestroika* and *glasnost* appeared to open up hopeful prospects for the just satisfaction of all manner of formerly ignored claims whether cultural, territorial or even secessionist.

On 5 March 1987, it was a geologist and a member of the Communist Party, Suren Aivazian, who, in a long letter addressed to Gorbachev, again raised the problem of attaching Nakhichevan and

Karabagh to Armenia.[103] He pointed out the anti-Armenian role played by Haidar Aliev, an Azeri from Nakhichevan, First Secretary of the Azeri Communist Party, who had risen quickly in the Soviet hierarchy thanks to his servile attitude towards Brezhnev. A few months later, another step was taken. A petition, drafted by the Armenian Academy of Sciences, addressed to Gorbachev in 1987, obtained several hundred thousand signatures. This petition focused on the idea of Azerbaijan being a 'Turkish Fifth Column in the USSR', and stressed the fact that Azerbaijan was aiming to get rid not only of the Armenians, but also of the Russians. After this came declarations by prominent Armenian personalities. In September 1987, the writer Zori Balayan, a native of Karabagh, asked his colleagues 'Ought we to keep silent?' The following month, the historian Sergei Mikoyan (son of Anastas Mikoyan) stated his views in public. In November, Abel Aghanbegian, the leading economist, and personal advisor to Gorbachev, questioned when passing through Paris declared: 'I would like to hear that Karabagh has become Armenian again. As an economist, I think it has more links with Armenia than with Azerbaijan. I have made a proposal to this effect. I hope that this problem will be solved in accordance with perestroika and democracy'.[104]

At the same time, from 1987 onwards, appeals and letters, both individual and collective, were sent off, in large numbers, to the authorities in Moscow; some individuals even instituted legal proceedings. In October 1987, six Armenians from the disputed regions accused the Baku authorities of having 'perpetrated genocide against the Armenian population between 1920 and 1987'. Aliev, the strong man of Azerbaijan, was likewise accused, of 'violating national and racial equality', in a letter addressed to the public prosecutor of the USSR by two Armenians, one of whom was a young economist, a native of Baku, Igor Muradian, soon to become an important figure.

At the end of 1987, events occurring in the village of Chardakhlu, in the Shamkhor district, to the north-west of Mountainous Karabagh (but outside the frontiers of the Autonomous Region) had important repercussions, in view of the prestige attaching to this region as the birthplace of two Soviet marshals, Babajanian and Baghramian. The First Secretary of the district, Asadov, had been trying for several months to drive out the Armenian population. A delegation sent to Moscow in protest returned empty-handed. On 30 November, Asadov appeared in the village with his militia, and deposed the Armenian director of the local state farm; there was a violent affray, lasting three hours. On 2 December, Asadov tried to force the inhabitants of the village to take part in a ceremony he was organizing to celebrate the 90th birthday of Baghramian; but they refused to be 'rehabilitated' for this purpose. The villages continued to be persecuted by other means, such as a blockade. But the Azeris, by this time, had lost one of their strongest man: Aliev, too compromised by his pro-Brezhnev stance, had been removed from office, although this did not prevent him from using his numerous contacts in order to keep control of affairs. In Yerevan itself, tension increased steadily, with more demonstrations organized more and more by well-known personalities, such as the two women poets Sylva Kaputikian and Maro Markavian, or by Victor Hambardzumian, the President of the Academy of Sciences.

# 14

## THE STRUGGLE FOR UNIFICATION: 1988 ONWARDS

For all Armenians, 1988 will be remembered as a 'crazy year', a year in which all goals appeared achievable, until the horrific earthquake in December. One Karabagh delegation after another went to Moscow, there were numerous meetings in the Autonomous Region, accompanied by many anti-Armenian attacks. 'Mountainous Karabagh is literally in a state of siege' announced a news reporter on the Armenian radio at the end of February. At the same time, the Azeri leaders refused to change their uncompromising stance, as expressed by their puppet, Boris Kevorkov: 'We shall die rather than relinquish Karabagh' – meaning 'we Azeris'.

This position was not echoed by the deputies of the regional soviet of Karabagh, even though they had been appointed by the 'system'. They were soon to take an historic step: on 20 February this soviet, at an extraordinary session, adopted a resolution calling on the soviets of Azerbaijan and Armenia to make every effort to reach 'a positive decision concerning the transfer of the region from the SSR of Azerbaijan to the SSR of Armenia'. This was a real bombshell, particularly since Bagirov, the First Secretary of the Azeri Communist Party, was present, yet was powerless to prevent the adoption of this resolution, which at last gave the Armenian claims a legal basis, in the Soviet sense of the term. Out of a total of 140 Armenian deputies, 110 voted for the resolution.

The news was greeted with rejoicing in Yerevan, where the first 'Karabagh Committee' was set up, under the direction of some 15 members, including Sylva Kaputikian, Victor Hambardzumian, Igor Muradian, Vazgen Manukian and others, who gradually assumed the leadership of political life in Yerevan. They little by little added other problems to Karabagh's claims: language, pollution, democratization, official recognition of 24 April for commemoration of the 1915 genocide, and of 28 May for commemoration of the creation of the Republic of Armenia in 1918 (spurned hitherto because of its 'Dashnak' flavour). The week of 20-27 February saw a series of huge demonstrations in front of the Opera House in Yerevan, infuriated by the negative replies of the First Secretary of the Armenian Communist Party, Karen Demirjian on the 22 February (the changes demanded 'run counter to the interests of the workers of the Armenian and the Azerbaijani SSR') and also of the Central Committee of the Communist Party of the USSR (who gave the same reply, with the addition of threats against the 'irresponsible extremists'). The population placed its hopes in Gorbachev, whose portrait was displayed everywhere. Strikes in Armenia, skirmishes in Karabagh: Sylva Kaputikian and Zori Balayan went to Moscow to meet Gorbachev, who asked for a month in which to bring about 'a new renaissance for Karabagh'. It was, therefore, decided to stop demonstrations for a month, and to meet again on 26 March. Meantime, Kevorkov was dismissed on 23 February from his post of director of the Communist Party of Karabagh, and replaced by Henrik Poghosian, who was perceived as the most courageous and most popular of all the Armenian political leaders.

And then, at the end of February came Sumgait. For three days between 27 and 29 February, this dormitory town in the suburbs of Baku became the scene of massacres, 'Armenian baiting', and murder, all unpunished in a way reminiscent of the attitude of the Russian authorities at the time of the pogroms in 1905. The official figure of 32 dead is derisory, and the evidence of eyewitnesses conclusive. In a long open letter dated 5 April, Sylva Kaputikian was to write: 'This massacre which, as everything showed, had been carefully planned beforehand... met with no resistance on the part of the local bodies responsible for keeping order; this massacre is a disgrace not only to Azerbaijan, but also to the whole of the USSR'. A parody of a trial, held discreetly in November, neither punished any culprits nor took any steps in order to establish the facts, though it sentenced one lowly functionary, Ahmed Ahmedov, to death.

The Sumgait drama received world-wide publicity and was a terrible shock to all Armenian communities, reviving memories of 1915. Indeed it was to the monument to the victims of the 1915 genocide that, on 8 March, a vast crowd of several hundred thousand Armenians flocked to pay homage to the victims of this new pogrom. Sumgait was seen as being the first step towards the liquidation of the presence of the half-million Armenians in Azerbaijan, a community who had been resident there for centuries. Failing attachment to Armenia, Mountainous Karabagh asked at least to be attached to the Russian Federation – anywhere rather than Azerbaijan. Karabagh also pointed out the responsibility of the Armenian SSR which, it was said, did not take a firm enough stand. Igor Muradian criticized the Soviet media, 'which are patently at a loss in this situation', the Azeri authorities who continued to incite massacres although the Armenians had stopped demonstrating, and also 'a number of the leaders of the Central Committee of the Soviet Communist Party' for 'their refusal to recognize the existence of national problems in the USSR, and to deal with them in time'.

During the month of March, the atmosphere grew more tense in Yerevan, where troops arrived. Various signs suggested that no positive decision would be taken by the Kremlin. Thus, the Institute of Oriental Studies in Moscow, instructed by the Communist Party of the Soviet Union to consider the problem, came to the following conclusions, disquieting because they might well have come straight from Baku: 'The Commission must, as far as possible, drag out the examination of this question. It is not desirable that Karabagh be attached to Armenia. An attempt must be made to calm down the population in the cultural and social spheres, and in day-to-day matters; to sacrifice some of the leaders if necessary and also of course, to find culprits of lesser rank. However, Mountainous Karabagh must not be attached to Armenia. It is now essential to create the impression of total 'glasnost', not as in the preceding period; and to publicize every minor clash between Armenians and Azerbaijanis, always putting the blame on the former. Steps must be taken to infiltrate Armenian circles, using for instance for this purpose the Kurds, who are the most friendly to the Armenians of all those living on Armenian territory, and so at the same time trying to undermine the friendly relations between the two.'[105]

On 21 March, *Pravda* published an article recognizing the deficiencies of the administration of Karabagh – putting the blame on Kevorkov – but stigmatizing the 'nationalist demonstrations' which, it said, 'would not affect the friendship between the Azerbaijan and Armenian peoples'. One of the three 'authors', Arakelian, the *Pravda* correspondent in Armenia, criticized this article and denounced this manoeuvre 'necessary to the Central Committee of the Communist Party of the USSR'. He was dismissed from his post a few days later.

The decision of the Presidium of the Supreme Soviet of the USSR, announced on 23 March 1988, though expected, came as a thunderbolt: a strong denial of re-attachment speaking of 'impermissible pressure', threatening legal action, and condemning 'all nationalist and extremist demonstrations'. Although a number of economic and cultural measures were decreed, they could not lessen the effect of the refusal. The full resolution is quoted as Document 3. Those Armenians who had hoped for change through perestroika were completely disillusioned and for them it was the end of the 'Gorbachev myth'. The leadership of the movement changed hands, Sylva Kaputikian being replaced, for two months, by Igor Muradian, who had no illusions about the 'other camp'. Yerevan was for one day a 'dead town', encircled by the army. A few days later, the troops withdrew from the town.

On 24 April, the anniversary of the commemoration of the 1915 genocide, the students of the University installed a *khachkar* – cross inscribed in stone – to the memory of Sumgait, next to the monument to the 1915 genocide on a hill overlooking Yerevan. Strikes and demonstrations continued. On 21 May, Moscow announced the simultaneous dismissal of the First Secretaries of the Azeri and Armenian Communist Parties, who were to be replaced by Abdul-Rahman Vezirov and Suren Harutiunian, respectively. Another commemoration was soon due – that of the 70th anniversary of the foundation of the Armenian Republic, with its tricolour red-blue-orange flag. (The official Soviet Armenian flag was red-blue-red.) This was regarded, wrongly, as 'Dashnak' – and therefore a provocation. It was impossible, in 1988, to prevent the population from celebrating the 28th of May by waving the original Armenian flag. The flags changed, the portraits also; Andranik replaced Gorbachev.

## The Karabagh Committee

It was in June 1988 that the 'Karabagh Committee', henceforth called 'Committee of Armenia for the Karabagh Movement', took final shape. It was formed of 11 intellectuals, scientists and writers, all (with one exception) aged 35-45. Igor Muradian had been removed and replaced by this Committee with its collective outlook and shared functions. Gradually this 'Committee', which had the support of the overwhelming majority of the population, became a *de facto* opposition, controlling political affairs by regular meetings attended by the crowd in the square in front of the Opera. The month of June was marked by demonstrations in Baku, against which tanks were used; on 13 June, the Azeri Soviet rejected the 20th February decision. There was also an intensification of Azeri attacks on the convoys passing between Armenia and Karabagh: the road running through Lachin became more and more dangerous and so was gradually abandoned, and use was made of the northern route, which was longer but patrolled by the army.

On 15 June, the Armenian Supreme Soviet voted unanimously for the re-attachment of Karabagh to Armenia – a decision countered two days later by a decision of the Supreme Soviet of Azerbaijan, whose consent was legally required. But it was on 28 June that there came a second reversal, after that of 23 March when Gorbachev, at the Nine-teenth Conference of the Communist Party held in Moscow, ruled out all possibility of frontiers being modified. Armenia replied by staging a general strike and on 5 July, occupying the Zvartnots airport just out-side Yerevan. The Soviet Army determinedly repressed the demonstra-tions, killing one person, whose funeral was the occasion for another large demonstration.

A third important date was approaching: on 18 July, the Karabagh question was again to be examined by the Presidium of the Supreme Soviet in Moscow. Previously, on 12 July, the Soviet of Mountainous Karabagh had adopted an unilateral decision to secede from Baku, a decision without precedent in Soviet history. A few days later, the Karabagh Committee called on the population to suspend the strike, pending the decision of Moscow. There was a third disappointment: another refusal on the question of the re-attachment. Moreover, the Presidium demanded that the situation be 'normalized'. Clearly there was nothing further that Armenians could expect from Moscow.

Within Armenia, the Karabagh Committee had succeeded in keep-ing within the 'legal' limits and keeping order within its ranks. Its meetings were a model of democracy. Meanwhile, there were constant skirmishes in Azerbaijan, and particularly in Karabagh, paralysed by the strike and then patrolled by the army which, at the end of Septem-ber, also appeared in Yerevan for several days. In September-October 1988, the population flocked in increasing numbers to the public meetings; and the 11 members of the Committee were unofficially rec-ognized as spokesmen for the Party and the government, dealing not only with the problems of Karabagh, but also with all those concern-ing Armenia.

The crucial period for the movement was the month of November. On the 7 October, the anniversary of the 1917 October Revolution, the 'dual power' was evident in Lenin Square, Yerevan, when, at the offi-cial ceremony, the Armenian Communist Party leaders spoke from the platform, the members of the Karabagh Committee from the street. During this extraordinary demonstration, the crowds, brandishing aloft tricolour flags, showed clearly which side they supported; and it was probably then that the authorities realized they must strike hard if they wanted to remain in office. On 22 November the Armenian Supreme Soviet met in session, with two new members: one member of the Karabagh Committee, Ashot Manucharian, and one person closely allied with the Karabagh Committee, Khachik Stambultsian. Fearing that some parliamentarians might be persuaded to change sides, the authorities suspended the session indefinitely at the end of the first day. From that moment onwards, events moved rapidly. Two days later the Karabagh Committee, legally, convened a quorum of the Soviet at the Opera House. The Karabagh Committee's programme was adopted. The government replied by proclaiming a State of Emergency promulgated during this session; the same session which the next day it declared, to be 'illegal'.

During this time in Azerbaijan a new tragedy was preparing at Kirovabad, the second largest city, the former Gandzak or Elizavetpol. The 40,000 Armenians living there originated from a very old historical settlement; most lived in one district of the town. Little was to be known about this 'new Sumgait', launched on 21 November, since the Armenian government authorities censored all information about it. Yet times had changed and the almost 200,000 Armenian refugees arriving from Azerbaijan had paid the price. The Azeris living in Armenia, less numerous, began a move in the opposite direction.

The end of the year 1988 was marked by a massive tragedy, the earthquake of 7 December. The Karabagh Committee dealt with the problem of aid to the victims, attempting to make up for the shortcomings of the authorities who were powerless. Gorbachev, who visited the earthquake area, said of Karabagh: 'The problem of Karabagh is being exploited by dishonest people, political demagogues, adventurers and – even worse – corrupt characters... We are about to strike out at all this riff-raff'.[106] Action followed quickly. In three 'round-ups' (10 and 24 December 1988, 7 January 1989) the 11 members of the Karabagh Committee were arrested, together with Igor Muradian, Khachik Stambultsian and Arkadi Manucharov. Detained in secret in Moscow, they were all, except the last-named, set free on 31 May 1989. Contrary to the hopes of the authorities, the result was to increase their popularity.

## Deadlock

On 12 January 1989, a decision was at last taken on the modification of the status of Karabagh: the USSR Supreme Soviet decided to confer on the Autonomous Region, provisionally, a 'special administrative status'. It was to remain part of Azerbaijan, but to be dependent on administration directly from Moscow, which appointed Arkadi Volsky as a 'Viceroy' in Karabagh. The advantage of this arrangement was obviously to free the Armenians of Mountainous Karabagh from the arbitrary rule of Baku. However, under this arrangement, the inhabitants of Karabagh had practically no say in the administration of the territory; there was no regional Soviet, only a Council, with purely formal powers, representing all nationalities. Poghosian, who had enjoyed great popularity, was henceforth only a deputy of the Supreme Soviet.

At the end of three months, a report on the new administration was submitted to Gorbachev by the top officials of the Communist Party and the executive committees of the districts of Mountainous Karabagh. The text of this report was disappointing to Armenians:

'We are obliged to note that the hopes of the Armenian population of the Autonomous Region have not been realized... Even the introduction of a special form of administration has not guaranteed the Armenian population against gross and shameless interference by Azerbaijan. Even worse, it looks as if the special Administration Committee has adopted the policy of aiding the authorities of the republic to 'Azerbaijanize' the region... Steps are being taken to accelerate the installation of Azerbaijani villages... In the Armenian villages, on the other hand, no work is being done,... The people of Mountainous Karabagh are indignant at the provocative statements made by Vezirov [the Azerbaijani leader], and the indulgent attitude of the Central Committee of the USSR Communist Party towards the authorities of the Republic... The best solution was and continues to be reunification with Armenia'.

The situation in Karabagh continued to be tense with strikes continuing. Imposed a year too late, at a time when Baku was in practice acting autonomously without reference to Moscow, the 'direct administration system' was bound to come to grief. It was officially abolished on 28 November 1989 and replaced by a military administration system attempting by various means to push the Autonomous Region back into the 'Azeri sphere'.

The year 1989 witnessed fundamental changes in Armenia. The Karabagh Committee became part of a vast 'Armenian National Movement' officially recognized by the authorities of the Republic. The authorities themselves totally changed their policy, supporting the claims of Karabagh to unification even to the point of proclaiming, on 20 February 1990, the decision of 5 July 1921 to be null and void. Thus the differences between the political factions became increasingly accentuated.

The same was true even on the geographical level; with the flow of refugees in both directions, the 1923 frontiers tended to form the dividing line between the different ethnic groups. More and more clashes occurred, particularly since there was no shortage of weapons. The pogroms in Baku at the beginning of 1990 finally drove Armenians out of the former oil capital. Armenia itself was mercilessly economically blockaded, its transport links through Azerbaijan were cut, and the Armenian villages north of the Autonomous Region have endured severe restrictions and hardship. The village of Getashen is under siege and the people survive through helicopter relief flights organized by the Armenian government. The population of the village of Kamo has been driven out.

Since November 1989 Mountainous Karabagh has been ruled from Baku and the Azerbaijani authorities there are doing all that they can to make life impossible for the population, with the apparent aim of driving them out and re-populating the territory with Azerbaijanis. In July 1990 the Second Secretary of the Azerbaijan Communist Party seriously formulated a plan for deporting all Armenians from Nagorno Karabagh – a grisly echo of the 1915 massacres. The Azeris have employed every means to isolate Mountainous Karabagh.

A vivid account of conditions was given by Alice Kelikian, an Armenian-American who was smuggled into Karabagh.[107] She recounted that the only petrol available was from Soviet soldiers selling at inflated prices, that almost all food was scarce apart from cabbage and dried herbs, that meat was rationed to one kilo per month although this was not available in government stores because of transport difficulties and because of Azeri raids on livestock kept by Armenians. The Armenian TV station had been blacked out for almost a year and communication with the outside world was limited to shortwave radio. About 26,000 Armenian refugees from Azerbaijan had fled to Karabagh, placing great strain on the education system. Most of the refugees are skilled workers and professionals from the cities and there is little employment for them in Karabagh. Although 6000 Soviet troops are based in Karabagh, they do not act to protect Armenians. During her short visit Alice Kelikian reported that two Armenians were murdered by Azeris while an Armenian partisan militia ambushed and killed three Soviet soldiers and an Azeri journalist. Because Armenian weapons legally held are confiscated by the authorities, the partisan militias rely on contraband weapons.

Azerbaijan was in a strong position in regard to Armenian Mountainous Karabagh which, though isolated, was increasingly determined not to submit to the Baku authorities: after all these pogroms and persecutions, unification with Armenia was seen, more than ever, to be the only solution to the Karabagh problem. But it was a solution that Azerbaijan was less ready than ever to accept. Things were back to a situation reminiscent of that existing in 1919. A complete deadlock appeared to have been reached.

## DOCUMENT 3

### Resolution of the Presidium of the Supreme Soviet of the USSR refusing the Re-attachment of Mountainous Karabagh to Armenia (23 March 1988)

On 23 March 1988, the USSR Supreme Soviet examined the situation in Mountainous Karabagh, in the SSR of Azerbaijan and the SSR of Armenia. On the basis of Article 81 of the USSR Constitution, the Presidium of the Supreme Soviet decided:

1. To stress that the situation of the SSR of Azerbaijan and the SSR of Armenia, in relation to events in Mountainous Karabagh, is harmful to the peoples of those republics and also, in general, to the continuing reinforcement of friendly relations between the peoples of the USSR, an unique multinational federal state. To consider it inadmissable to strive to solve complex national and territorial problems by exercising pressure on the organs of state power in an atmosphere marked by the exacerbation of emotions and passions, whilst setting up all kinds of illegal bodies proposing the changing of the state and administrative boundaries laid down in the USSR constitution, with consequences impossible to foresee. Resolutely to condemn criminal acts by certain groups and certain persons, which have resulted in victims; and to take account of the fact that administrative and penal proceedings have been instituted against the culprits.

2. In accordance with the resolutions of the 27th Congress of the party and of the plenary sessions of the Central Committee of the Communist Party of the Soviet Union held thereafter and with the appeal of Mikhail Gorbachev, General Secretary of the Central Committee of the Communist Party of the USSR, calling on the workers, the peoples of Azerbaijan and Armenia, it is the responsibility of the Soviets of people's deputies of the SSR of Armenia and Azerbaijan radically to improve their mass political and educational work amongst the population, always using Leninist principles as the basis for the nationalities policy and for friendship and unity between the peoples of the USSR; to make a profound analysis of all the reasons for the exacerbation of inter-ethnic relations; to eliminate such conflicts and to take energetic measures against all demonstrations of nationalism and extremism; to create a calm and constructive atmosphere in enterprises and educational establishments by mobilizing the efforts of the workers of all the nationalities of ethnic groups inhabiting these republics, with a view to bringing about the revolutionary changes now being made in our society.

3. It is incumbent on the Presidium of the Supreme Soviet of the Azerbaijan SSR and the Presidium of the Supreme Soviet of the Armenian SSR to take concerted measures to reinforce socialist legality and public order, to protect the legitimate interests of citizens of all nationalities, and to take severe measures against all persons committing acts designed to destabilize the situation, to the detriment of friendship and cooperation between brother Soviet nations.

4. It is incumbent on the USSR Council of Ministers to adopt measures designed to solve the urgent problems of the economic, social and cultural development of the autonomous Region of Mountainous Karabagh.

5. The USSR Department of the Public Prosecutor and the USSR Ministry of the Interior are enjoined to take all measures requisite to assure public order and protect the legitimate interests of the populations of the SSR of Azerbaijan and of Armenia.

> Tass, 23 March 1988, reproduced in the bulletin
> *Soviet News*, No. 776 of 30 March 1988

# CONCLUSION

# LOOKING TO THE FUTURE

The situation of the Armenian people has changed radically since the introduction of perestroika in 1985 and the later ending of central one-party control throughout the USSR. It is impossible for conditions in Armenia to return to what they had been in the pre-Gorbachev era, without massive shedding of blood.

There have been some gains since 1985, notably the freeing of politics, journalism and historical discourse within Armenia. But for Armenia there has been perhaps more negative features. In the first place, there has been the very slow response to the disastrous earthquake of 7 December 1988, in which an estimated 28,000 people died – a natural catastrophe, which was also a national one. Rebuilding is continuing painfully slowly and people from the disaster area have had to spend two icy winters under army canvas or in temporary metal shelters, which are freezing in winter and baking in summer. Considerable amounts of money, donated to Armenians and funnelled through the Moscow Narodny Bank, never reached Spitak and Leninakan. (However, all donations sent through 'Aid Armenia' have reached their destination.)

Secondly, the situation for the people in Nagorno Karabagh is deadlocked, and shows no sign of improvement. The brutal and inhuman campaign being waged against these Armenian villagers by the authorities of both Moscow and Baku has continued, a bizarre and repellent anti-democratic colonial dictatorship. Azerbaijan has stopped short of full-scale invasion and eviction, but one wonders for how long – and also if it happened, who, apart from Armenians themselves, would make any protests.

The Western powers have been remarkably silent on the issue of democratic rights for the people of Nagorno Karabagh, despite much righteous anger about the Baltic issues. No official or semi-official Westerner has ever addressed the issue of the nature of ideological Turkism towards the Armenian people who still live as a majority in their own land. It is possible that the silence on Karabagh occurs as a result of interests in Turkey, a state which has no interest in supporting democratic government within Karabagh but only for Azerbaijan's dictatorship (and consequent denial of human rights) to continue.

The future for Mountainous Karabagh has thus become part of the future of the Armenian nation as a whole, and cannot be separated from it. Yet on another level, it is clearly a local problem which needs specific and local solutions. Despite 70 years of harassment and depopulation policies, Armenians still constitute a majority in Mountainous Karabagh, and it is clearly their wish to be unified with the newly renamed Republic of Armenia. As is the ideal in all democratic societies, the wishes of the majority should be observed. This means not only unification but also that there must be full recognition of Armenian language, education and culture, including urgent attempts to preserve ancient monuments.

Nevertheless, there are also minorities whose human rights need to be considered. There are substantial Azeri populations within Karabagh, some of whom are historic communities. They must have guaranteed rights to their language and culture also. Such rights must also be guaranteed to the Kurds in and around Lachin, whose distrust of and suppression by the Azerbaijani government has promoted their movement to unify with 'Christian' Armenia rather than 'Muslim' Azerbaijan.

What is very doubtful is whether Nakhichevan can follow the Karabagh path of unification. Its position has always been more ambiguous than Karabagh – even at the beginning of the 20th Century it had a mixed population of Armenians, Turkish-Tatars and Kurds. What is certain is that the Armenian minority has been almost completely expelled as a result of Azeri policies and while it inhabited the territory its minority rights were not protected.

Thirdly, there is the issue of the economy. This has suffered in Armenia, partly as a result of the disastrous performance of the economy throughout the USSR since the advent of perestroika, and more especially because of the blockade imposed upon Armenia by Azerbaijan. As a result there is a very severe fuel shortage, and food is often in short supply. Again, this matter seldom reaches the headlines of the newspapers, yet it amounts to a virtual act of war against the Armenian people. The President of the Armenian Republic, Levon Ter Petrosian, has said that his people are self-reliant, and capable with dealing with hardships; one must hope that he is right.

As regards Turko-Armenian relations, it may be that economic realities compel Armenians to trade with Turkey. There are several issues here which need to be examined. In the first place, there is a danger that relations once started may be stopped arbitrarily by Turkey. Armenia would then be little more than a weak protectorate, like that envisaged by the never-implemented Treaty of Alexandropol (December 1920). Moreover, the harsh and domineering tone of Turkey does not augur well for relations based on equality. Turkey seems only capable of adopting an attitude of superiority, never of equality. The country seems to have a collective problem about being seen to be powerful and macho. Articles that appear in the Turkish press about Armenians (such as that in *Milliyet* of 19 November 1990, by Coskun Kirca) adopt a brutal, threatening and anti-democratic tone, as if wishing to reinforce negative Western stereotypes of the terrible Turk.

As regards the Armenian past, it would unquestionably make for a healthier international climate if Turkey accepted that the former Istanbul administration had committed a war crime against the Armenian people in 1915. At the present time, the Turkish government is pursuing an opposite policy; the events of 1915 are seen in Ankara as civil war, and attempts are made by the Turks to portray the Armenians as perpetrators and not victims. This is historical fantasy, but nevertheless for Turkey at the moment, it is apparently a necessary fantasy.

Within Turkey in the late 1980s, there was improvement in the communal conditions of the Armenians in Istanbul. But problems remain severe, and there are many small bureaucratic ways in which the government is squeezing the Armenian minority. The continued existence of Armenian schools in Istanbul remains an area of concern; and also the preservation of Armenian monuments in eastern Turkey which, despite being financially beneficial tourist attractions for Turkey's depressed eastern provinces, are allowed to fall into disrepair to satisfy the ideological hatred and extremism of ruling circles. In the 1980s the Armenian Patriarch was forbidden to celebrate mass in the Church at Aghtamar. Such simple denials of religious rights are hardly persuasive advocacy for Turkey's membership of the European Community.

Armenian terrorism is no longer an issue, as the Armenian people have discovered that legitimate advocacy of their cause advances the process better than illegitimate prosecution of it. The advances made by their community by legitimate means both in Europe and the United States, have increased awareness of the Armenian case far more effectively than terrorism, which has been shown to actually hinder the Armenian cause.

The near-independence achieved by the Republic of Armenia, and the persuasive, undramatic manner in which the new non-Communist government has begun to reclaim Armenia's position on the world stage, has impressed many. Much is still uncertain (notably whether the USSR will lurch back into reaction and military crack-down), but the patient, unadventurist determination that the government has shown will undoubtedly be of benefit to both the people of Armenia and to their fellow Armenians of Nagorno Karabagh who are suffering from extreme discrimination, harassment and denial of many basic human rights. The tone coming from Yerevan (in February 1991) is one of pragmatism and seriousness.

Above all, Armenia would seem to need, new treaties with Moscow and with her neighbours, economic normalization, and, eventually, representation in the United Nations. Some of these may lie some way in the future. But the Armenian people are patient and resourceful; they have waited a long time for things which most nations take for granted, and will doubtless wait a little longer.

# Footnotes

1   Summarized by Deukmejian, in *Soviet Studies*, Glasgow University 1968.
2   See Dadrian, V.N., articles in the *International Journal of Middle East Studies*, 1986 and the *Yale Journal of International Law*, 1989.
3   See Housepian, M., *Smyrna 1922: The Destruction of a City*.
4   See Walker, C.J., article in *The Times*, 5/9/74.
5   See *The Armenian Observer*, 2/6/76.
6   See the articles by Dadrian, V.N., *op. cit.* as note 1.
7   See *The Economist*, 19/1/91.
8   *Ibid.*
9   Many of the figures used in this chapter come from an article in *Hairenik Dzain* ('The Voice of the Homeland'), Armenian weekly, Yerevan, 31/10/90. For *Lebanon* see also McDowall, D., Lebanon, MRG Report, 1989.
10  Full particulars are given in the article on the Armenian SSR in the latest *Encyclopaedia Brittanica*, written by a Soviet scholar, Dr. A.A. Mints.
11  Figures from the Russian-language *Bulletin of Statistics* (Moscow, 1980) and *USSR Population Census for 1984* (1985).
12  The name 'Karabagh' appears for the first time in a Georgian chronicle dating from the 14th Century: *Georgian Chronicle 1207-1318*, translated into Armenian by Mouradian, P., Yerevan, 1971, p.112. See also *Kartlis Tskhovreba*, in Georgian, (trans. 'History of Georgia'), vol. II, Tbilisi, 1959, p.240. This name is also mentioned by a 14th Century Persian historian: Hamd-Allah Mustawi of Gazwin, *The Geographical Part of the Nuzhat-al-Qulub*, trans. by le Strange, G., Leyden, 1919, pp. 173-174. It appears to be derived from the Persian phrase *'bag-i-siyah'* (meaning 'black garden'), but it is not known for certain to what the epithet 'black' refers.
13  For the study of the historical geography of ancient Armenia there are various sources, including the Armenian Atlas of the World, or *Ashkharhatsouits* compiled in the 7th Century (French trans. *'Geographie de Moise de Corene'*) by Soukry, A., Venice, 1881. It was updated by Eremian, S., *Armenia According to Ashkharhatsouits*, Yerevan, 1963 (in Armenian). See also Hakopian, T., *Geographie Historique de l'Armenie*,

137

2nd edition, Yerevan 1968 (in Armenian).
14 Melikichvili, G., *Urartian Cuneiform Inscriptions*, Moscow, 1960, p.310; No.161 and p.446 (in Russian).
15 Strabo, *Geography*, vol.XI, chap.14, 4; Loeb edition, vol. 5, pp.320 ff.
16 Khorenatsi, Movses (Moses of Khoren), *History of the Armenians*, vol. II; chap. 44-45 (English trans. by Thomson, R., Cambridge, Mass., and London, 1978, pp. 180-185.)
17 Strabo, *op. cit.*, vol. XI, chap. 14, 5; Loeb edition, vol. 5, p.325.
18 Aliev, K., *Caucasian Albania, 1st Century BC to 1st Century AD*, Baku, 1974 (in Russian); Buniyatov, Z., *Azerbaijan in the 7th-9th Centuries*, Baku, 1965 (in Russian); Mamedova, F., *Political History and Historical Geography of Caucasian Albania*, Baku, 1986 (in Russian).
19 These sources are examined in: Mnatasakanian, A., *On the Literature of the Country of the Aghouanks*, Yerevan, 1966, pp. 31-35 (in Armenian); Anassian, H., 'Report on Caucasian Albania', in *Revue des Etudes Armeniennes*, (*REArm N.S.*), vol. VI, Paris, 1969, pp.303-305; and, in particular, Akopian, A., *Albania...* (op.cit.) pp.21-27 and 96-98. Cf. Strabo, XI, 14, 4; Pliny the Elder, *Natural History*, book VI, chap. 15 (Loeb edition, vol. 2); Plutarch, *Lives*, vol. VII, Pompey, chap.34, 1-4; Ptolemy, *Geography*, book V, chap.12; Dio Cassius, *Roman History*, book XXXVI (Loeb edition, vol. 3, pp.92-3); Agathangelos, *History of the Armenians*, chap. 28 and 795 (French trans. in Langlois, V. *Collection des historiens...de l'Armenie*, vol.1, Paris, 1867, pp.119 and 171); Buzand, P., *Histoire de l'Armenie*, book III, chap. 7 and book V, chap. 13 (French trans. in Langlos, pp. 215 and 288); Ashkharhatsouits, *Geographie de Moise de Corene*, book V, chap. 21 (trans. Soukry, A. Venice, 1881, p.39).
20 A summary of these points is found in Ulubabian, B., *Studies on the History of the Eastern Part of Armenia (5th-7th Centuries)*, Yerevan, 1981 (in Armenian); and Akopian, A., op.cit. Cf. Author's report on the work of Akopian, A., to appear in *REArm N.S.*, vol.XXI.
21 On the Arranshahik dynasty, see Ulubabian, B., *op.cit.*, pp.129-197.
22 Daskhurantsi (or Kaghankatvatsi), M., *Histoire de l'Albanie (Aghouank)*, book III, chap.23 (English trans. by Dowsett, C., London, 1961).
23 On this monument, see Hasratian, M., 'L'ensemble architectural d'Amarass', in *REArm. N.S.*, vol. XII, Paris, 1977, pp. 243-259.
24 On the subject of these inscriptions and how to decipher them see Muraviev, S., 'Three Studies of Albanian Writing in the Caucasus' in *Annual of Ibero-Caucasian Linguistics*, VIII, Tiflis, 1981, pp.222-325 (in Russian).
25 Ulubabian, B., *op.cit.*, pp.73-79.
26 For a synthesis of the Armenian kingdoms in the 9th-11th Centuries, see Dedeyan, G., *Histoire des Armeniens*, Toulouse, 1982, pp.215-268.

[27] On Artsakh or Khachen after the Arab occupation, see Ulubabian, B., *The Principality of Khachen in the 10th-16th Centuries*, Yerevan, 1975, pp.62-112.

[28] Constantine Porphyrogenitus, *De Ceremoniis aulae Byzantinae*, book II, chap. 48 (Corpus Scriptorum Historiae Byzantinae, Constantinus Porphyrogenete, vol.1, Bonn., 1829, p.687).

[29] Akopian, A., *op.cit.*, pp.261-265.

[30] *Ibid.*, p.270.

[31] *Ibid.*, pp.270-271 and 276.

[32] See the works of Buniyatov, Z. and Mamedova, F. quoted in Note 7. This attempt at appropriation extended even to the cross-stones ('*khachkars*') to which certain art historians from Baku give the Turkified name '*khachdach*'. Compare the paper submitted by Akhudov, D. and M. (in Russian) at the Fourth International Symposium on Georgian Art, Tiflis, 1983.

[33] Ulubabian, B., *op. cit.*, pp.124-170.

[34] *Ibid.*, pp.171-217.

[35] Inscriptions collected by Barkhudarian, S., *Corpus Inscriptionum Armenicarum*, book V, 'Artsakh', Yerevan, 1982 (in Armenian). The most ancient known Armenian inscription from Mountainous Karabagh (inscription No.1, p.12) engraved on the base of a *khachkar*, is dated 853. It is to be found in the monastery of St. James of Metzirants, in the Martakert district.

[36] See, for example, Hasrat'yan, M. and Thierry, M., 'Le Couvent de Ganjasar', in *REArm. N.S.*, vol. XV, Paris, 1981, p.289-316; Thierry, J.M. and Donabedian, P., *Les Arts Armeniens*, Paris, 1987, p.526; Ulubabian, B. and Hasratian, M., *Gandzassar, Documenti di Architettura Armena*, No.17, Milan, 1987.

[37] Hasratian, M., 'Le complex monastique de Dadivank', in *Terzo Simposio Internazionale di Arte Armena*, 1981, Atti, Venice, 1984, pp.275-287; Thierry, J.M. and Donabedian, P., *op.cit.*, pp.511-512; Thierry, J.M. and Hasratyan, M., 'Dadivankeen Arc'ax', in *REArm. N.S.*, vol. XVI, Paris, 1982, pp.259-288. On the medieval architecture in Karabagh as a whole, see the works in Armenian (Yerevan, 1980 and 1982) and in Russian (Yerevan, 1988) of Mkrtitchian, C.; also, Lala Comneno, Cuneo, P. and Manukian, S., *Gharabagh*, Milan, 1988.

[38] Dedeyan, G. (Ed.), *History of the Armenians*, pp.377-384; Hewsen, R., 'The Meliks of Eastern Armenia', in *REArm N.S.*, vol. IX, Paris, 1972, pp.285-329 and vol. X, 1973-74, pp.281-303; Raffi, 'The Melikates of Khamsa,' in *Works*, vol. X, Yerevan, 1964 (in Armenian); Toumanoff, C., *Manual of Genealogy and Chronology of Christian Caucasia*, Rome, 1978.

39  Libaridian, G. (Ed.), *The Karabagh File, Documents and Facts, 1918-1988*, Zoryan Institute, Cambridge, 1988, p.3.

40  *History of the Armenian People*, vol. IV, Armenian Academy of Sciences, Yerevan, 1972 (in Armenian); *Armeno-Russian Relations in the First Third of the 18th Century* (collection of documents), vol. I and II, Yerevan, 1964 and 1967 (in Russian); Arutiunian, P., *The Liberation Movement of the Armenian People in the First Quarter of the 18th Century*, Moscow, 1954 (in Russian); Essefian, A., 'The Mission of Israel Ori for the Liberation of Armenia', in *Recent Studies in Modern Armenian History*, Cambridge, MA, 1972; Ezov, G., *Peter the Great's Relations with the Armenian People*, St. Petersburg, 1898 (in Russian); Johannisjan, A., *Israel Ori and the Armenian Liberation Movement*, Munich, 1913; Leo, *Works*, vol. III, book 2, Yerevan, 1973 (in Armenian).

41  *Encyclopedia of Islam*, first and second editions, Leiden-Paris, 1960, articles 'Arran' and 'Karabagh'.

42  Galoyan, G. (ed.), *Mountainous Karabagh, Historical Guide*, Armenian Academy of Sciences, Yerevan, 1988, p.13 (in Russian); Djevanchir, Mirza Djamal, *History of Karabagh*, Baku, 1959 (in Russian); Djevanchir, Ahmedbek, *The political existence of the Khanate of Karabagh*, Baku, 1961 (in Russian).

43  *Mountainous Karabagh, Historical Guide*, op.cit., pp. 16-17;  Schiltberger, J., *Journey in Europe, Asia and Africa from 1394 to 1427* (Russian trans.), published in Odessa in 1866 by Bruhn, P., re-published at Baku in 1984 by Bunyatov, Z.  Note that, in this re-publication, both the passage about Karabagh, 'situated in Armenia', and also the sentence 'where the Armenian villages are forced to pay tribute to the infidels' were deleted by the Azerbaijani publisher. An English translation has also been published by the Hakluyt Society (1897).

44  *Mountainous Karabagh, Historical Guide*, op.cit., p.18.

45  Youzefovitch, T., *The Treaties Concluded by Russia with the East: Political and Economic Treaties*, St. Petersburg, 1869, pp. 208-214 (in Russian); Yoannissian, A., *The Attachment of Transcaucasia to Russia and International Relations at the Beginning of the 19th Century*, Yerevan, 1968 (in Russian).

46  Manoukian, S. and Vahramian, A., *Gharabagh Documenti*, Milan, 1988, p.47.

47  Libaridian, G. (Ed.), *op.cit.*

48  Mourier, J., *Guide au Caucase*, Paris, 1894, p.179; Chantre, B., *A Travers l'Armenie Russe*, Paris, 1893, p.45; Baedeker, K., *La Russie* (Third Edition), Leipzig, 1902, p.410.

49  Tavtian, R., 'Pages du passe de Chouchi', *Haratch* (Paris), 2/4/88; Ghazian, A., 'Chouchi', *Haireniki Dzain*, Erevan, 6/11/88; Haroutiouni-

an, C., *Short Chronology of the History of the Armenian People: 1801-1917* (in Armenian), Yerevan, 1955.
50  Varandian, M., *History of the Armenian Revolutionary Federation*, (in Armenian), vol. I, Paris, 1932, pp.389, 404; Villari, L., *Fire and Sword in the Caucasus*, London, 1906, p.198.
51  Walker, C.J., *Armenia, The Survival of a Nation*, London, 1980, p.76; Villari, pp. 203, 328; Varandian, pp.421, 430.
52  Ter Minassian, A., 'Particularites de la Revolution de 1905 en Transcaucasie' in *1905, La Premiere Revolution Russe*, Paris, 1986, p.329.
53  Varandian, *op.cit.*, p. 399.
54  Sevian, V., *Haratch* 18/3/88; Khatisian, A. *The Birth and Development of the Armenian Republic* (in Armenian), Athens, 1930, p.70.
55  Nassibian, A., *Britain and the Armenian Question*, London, 1984, p.100.
56  Ulubabian, B., *Haireniki Dzain*, 6/88; Messerlian, Z., *About the Armenian Question* (in Armenian), Beirut, 1978, p.132; Hovannisian, R., 'The Armeno-Azerbaijani Conflict over Mountainous Karabagh', in the *Armenian Review*, 24, Boston, 1971, p.9.
57  Abrahamian, H., *Haireniki Dzain*, 11/88; Hovannisian, K., *Haratch* 27/4/88; Messerlian, pp.132; Vratsian, S., *The Republic of Armenia* (in Armenian), Paris, 1928, p.281.
58  *Ibid.*, (all sources quoted).
59  Sevian, ibid.
60  Ellis, C., *The Transcaspian Episode*, London, 1963, p.21.
61  Abrahamian, H., *ibid.*; Vratsian, *ibid.*, p.282; Hovannisian, p.11.
62  Arslanian, A., *Haratch* 8/2/84. Khatisian, *ibid.*, p.153; Ter Minassian, A., *La Republique d'Armenie*, Brussels, 1989, p.133.
63  Libaridian (Ed.), *ibid.*, p.11.
64  Harutiunian, A., *The Turkish Intervention in Transcaucasia in 1918* (in Armenian), Yerevan, pp. 328; Abrahamanian, *Hair Dzain* 11/88; Avo, *Njdeh* (in Armenian), Beirut, 1968, pp.78.
65  Abrahamanian, *ibid.*
66  Libaridian, *ibid.*, p.16.
67  Hovannisian, *ibid.*, pp. 35; Vratsian, *ibid.*, pp. 291.
68  Libaridian, *ibid.*, p.156.
69  Sevian, *Haratch*, 19/3/88.
70  Libaridian, *ibid.*, p.25.
71  Sevian, *Haratch* 19/3/88; Khatissian, *ibid.*, p.169; Vratsian, *ibid.*, p.342.
72  Central Archives of the October Revolution in the USSR. Funds 130, File 4, Ch. 496, p.115.
73  Institute of Marxism-Leninism. CPSU Central Archives. Funds 2, File 14.516, p.2.
74  *Ibid.*, Funds 64, File 2, Ch. 5, p.19.

[75] *Ibid.*, Funds 2, File 14.516, p.2.

[76] Ulubabian, *ibid.*

[77] Institute of Marxism-Leninism. *Ibid.*, Funds 64, file 1, Ch. 10, pp. 9-10.

[78] Poidebard, A. 'La Transcaucasie et la republique d'Armenie dans les textes diplomatiques (1918-21)' in *REArm*, 4, 1924, pp.61.

[79] *Ibid.*, pp.70.

[80] Afanasyan, S., *L'Armenie, l'Azerbaidjan et la Georgie (1917-1923)*, Paris, 1981, p. 148.

[81] *Pravda*, 4/12/20

[82] *Ibid.*

[83] Poidebard, *ibid.*, pp. 74, 85.

[84] Sevian, *Haratch* 19/3/88; Mikaelian, V. and Khourchoudian, L., 'Historical Questions Related to Mountainous Karabagh' in *Lraber: Messager des Sciences Sociales*, Yerevan, April 1988, no.4 (544) (in Russian).

[85] Ulubabian, *op.cit.*

[86] *Ibid.*

[87] Mikaelian and Khourchoudian, *op.cit.*

[88] *Ibid.*

[89] *Le Dur Passe du Caucase*, Novosti, Moscow, 1988, pp. 10, 13.

[90] Libaridian, *op.cit.*, p. 38.

[91] Miridjian, G., *Haratch* 7/1/88.

[92] *L'Azerbaidjan*, Novosti, Moscow, 1981, p.12.

[93] *Mountainous Karabagh: A Historical Guide* (in Russian), Academy of Sciences of the Armenian SSR, Yerevan, 1988.

[94] *Glasnost*, No.1, Paris, February 1989, p. 90; Messerlian, *op.cit.*, p. 156.

[95] Rado, *Guide a travers l'Union Sovietique*, Berlin, 1929, p. 756; Mouradian, C., 'Le Probleme du Haut Karabagh'in *Slovo* 7, 1985, p.56.

[96] Rado, *op.cit.*, p.756.

[97] Avaguian, A., *Pages from the Cultural and Educational History of Mountainous Karabagh* (in Armenian), Yerevan, 1982.

[98] Khouabekian, V. and Assatratian, B., *Haireniki Dzain*, 1/6/88; Mouradian, *op.cit.*, p.64; Academy of Sciences of the Armenian SSR, op.cit., p.47; Barseghov, H., *The Right to Self-Determination...*, Yerevan, 1990, p.122.

[99] *Haratch*, 14/4/88.

[100] Hadjibeyli, T., 'La question du Haut-Karabagh. Une point de vue azerbaidjanais', in *Le Monde musulman a l'epreuve de la frontiere*, special number of *Revue du Monde Musulman et de Mediterranee*, no.48-49, Aix-en-Provence, 1988/2-3, p. 288.

[101] Unless otherwise indicated, the citations that follow come from *Libaridian*, *op.cit.*, Glasnost, op.cit. or *Artsakh*.

[102] Messerlian, *op.cit.*, pp.177.

[103] *Haratch*, 12/87.
[104] *Haratch*, 19/11/87.
[105] 'Violence dans l'Est Europeen', in *Etudes Polemologiaues*, No.46 (2/88); *Pensee Russe*, 18/3/88, Paris.
[106] *Notre malheur a tous, Armenie*, Novosti, Moscow, December 1988, p.10.
[107] *The Independent*, 21/1/91

# SELECT BIBLIOGRAPHY

AKOPIAN, A., *L'Albanie-Aghouank dans les sources greco-latines et armeniennes anciennes*, Yerevan, 1987 (in Russian).

ALAMUDDIN, I., *Papa Kuenzler and the Armenians*, London 1970.

ALLEN, W.E.D., and MURATOFF, P., *Caucasian Battlefields*, Cambridge,
1953.

ANDERSON, M.S., *The Eastern Question, 1774-1923*, London, 1966.

ANDONIAN, A., *Documents officiels concernant les massacres armeniens*,
Paris, 1920.

ARSLANIAN, A., 'Britain and the Armeno-Azerbaijani Struggle for Mountainous Karabagh 1918-1919,' in *Middle Eastern Studies (1)*, 1980, p.92.

BARDAKJIAN, Kevork B., *Hitler and the Armenian Genocide*, Cambridge,
Mass., 1985.

BRYCE, James, Viscount, *Transcaucasia and Ararat*, 4th ed., London, 1896.

BURNEY, Charles and LANG, D.M., *The Peoples of the Hills: Ancient Ararat
and Caucasus*, London and New York, 1971.

BUXTON, Noel and Harold, *Travels and Politics in Armenia*, London, 1914.

CARSWELL, John, *New Julfa: the Armenian Churches and other buildings*,
Oxford, 1968.

DADRIAN, Vahakn N., 'The Naim-Andonian Documents on the World
War I Destruction of the Ottoman Armenians: the Anatomy of a Genocide,' in *International Journal of Middle East Studies*, Vol.18, No.3 (August
1986), pp.311-360.

DADRIAN, Vahakn N., 'Genocide is a Problem of National and International Law: The World War I Armenian Case,' in *Yale Journal of International Law*, vol.14, No.2.(Summer 1989), pp.221-334.

DEDEYAN, G. (Ed.), *Histoire des Armeniens*, Toulouse, 1982.

DER NERSESSIAN, Sirarpie, *The Armenians*, London and New York, 1969.
*Encyclopedia of Islam*, 1st Ed. 'Turan'; 2nd Ed. 'Anadolu', 'Arminiyya'
etc.

GALOYAN, G., (Ed.), *Le Haut-Karabagh, memento historique*, Academie des
Sciences d'Armenie, Yerevan, 1988 (in Russian). Translation in English
and Armenian, Athens, 1988.

GIDNEY, James B., *A Mandate for Armenia*, Ohio, 1967.

GRAVES, Robert, Sir, *Storm Centres of the Near East: Personal Memories 1879-1919*, London, 1933.

*Great Soviet Encyclopedia* ('Bol'shaya Sovetskaya Entsiklopediya'), article 'Armenian SSR' and separate articles on Armenian places, cities and leading personalities. (The English Language edition of the entire encyclopedia was published in 1978).

HOSTLER, C.W., *Turkism and the Soviets*, London, 1957.

HOUSEPIAN, Marjorie, *Smyrna 1922: the Destruction of a City*, London, 1972.

HOVANNISIAN, Richard G., 'The Armeno-Azerbaijani conflict over Mountainous Karabagh, 1918-1919,' in *The Armenian Review* (24), 1971, Boston, pp.3-39.

HOVANNISIAN, Richard G., *Armenia on the Road to Independence, 1918*, London, 1967.

HOVANNISIAN, Richard G., *The Republic of Armenia*, Vol.I, 1918-1919, Los Angeles, 1971; Vol II, 1919-1920, Los Angeles, 1983.

KARABEKIR, Kazim, *Istiklal Harbimiz* ('Our War of Independence'), Istanbul, 1960 and 1969.

KAYALOFF, Jacques, *The Battle of Sardarabad*, The Hague and Paris, 1973.

KAZEMZADEH, Firuz, *The Struggle for Transcaucasia*, 1917-1921, New York and Oxford, 1951.

KRIKORIAN, Mesrob K., *Armenians in the Service of the Ottoman Empire*, 1860-1908, London, 1978.

LALA, Commeno M., CUNEO, P., MANOUKIAN, S., *Gharabagh*, Documenti di Architettura Armena, no.19, Milan, 1988.

LANG, D.M., *Armenia: Cradle of Civilisation*, 2nd Ed., London, 1978.

LEHMANN-HAUPT, C.F., *Armenien Einst und Jetzt*, 3 Vols., Berlin and Leipzig, 1910-1931.

LEPSIUS, Johannes, *Deutschland und Armenien*, 1914-1918, Potsdam, 1919.

LEWIS, Bernard, *The Emergence of Modern Turkey*, 2nd Ed., London, 1968.

LIBARIDIAN, G., (Ed.), *The Karabagh File*, Cambridge, Mass., 1988.

LUKE, Harry, Sir, *Cities and Men: an Autobiography*, Vol.2., London, 1953.

LYNCH, H.F.B., *Armenia: Travels and Studies*, 2 Vols., London, 1901, reprinted Beirut, 1965.

MATOSSIAN, Mary K., *The Impact of Soviet Policies in Armenia*, Leiden, 1962.

MKRTITCHIAN, C., *Les monuments historico-architecturaux du Haut-Karabagh*, Yerevan, 1st Ed. 1980, 2nd Ed. 1985 (in Armenian), 3rd Ed. 1988 (in Russian).

MORGENTHAU, Henry, *Secrets of the Bosphorus: Constantinople 1913-1916*, London, 1919. (Published in the USA with the title Ambassador Morgenthau's Story).

NALBANDIAN, Louise, *The Armenian Revolutionary Movement*, Los Angeles, 1963.

NASSIBIAN, Akaby, *Britain and the Armenian Question*, 1915-1923, London and New York, 1984.

NOVE, Alex and NEWTH, J.A., *The Soviet Middle East: a Model for Development?*, London, 1967.

ORMANIAN, Malachia, *The Church of Armenia*, new Ed., London, 1955.

PASTERMADJIAN, H., *Histoire de l'Armenie*, 2nd Ed., Paris, 1964.

PERMANENT PEOPLE'S TRIBUNAL, *A Crime of Silence: the Armenian Genocide*, London, 1985.

SALMASLIAN, A., *Bibliographie de l'Armenie*, 2nd Ed., Yerevan, 1969.

SANJIAN, Avedis K., *The Armenian Communities in Syria under Ottoman Dominion*, Cambridge, Mass., 1965.

SHIRAGIAN, Arshavir, *The Legacy: Memoirs of an Armenian Patriot*, Boston, Mass., 1976.

SUNY, Ronald G., (Ed.), *Transcaucasia: Nationalism and Social Change*, Ann Arbor, 1983.

SURMELIAN, Leon, *I Ask You, Ladies and Gentlemen*, London, 1946.

TABROZLI, A., *Histoire du Daglig (Haut)-Karabagh a la lumiere de documents historiques*, Strasbourg, 1989.

TERNON, Yves, *The Armenian Cause*, New York, 1985.

TORIGUIAN, Shavarsh, *The Armenian Question and International Law*, Beirut, 1973.

TOUMANOFF, Cyril, 'Armenia and Georgia' in *Cambridge Medieval History*, Vol, IV, Part I, 1966.

TOYNBEE, A.J., 'The Extermination of the Armenians', Chapter 133 of *The Times History of the War*, Vol. VIII, London, 1916.

TOYNBEE, A.J., (Ed.), *The Treatment of Armenians in the Ottoman Empire*, London, 1916. (Great Britain, Blue Book, Miscellaneous no.31 (1916); reprinted with a decoding appendix, Beirut, 1972.)

TOYNBEE, A.J., *Turkey: a Past and a Future*, London, 1917.

TRUMPENER, Ulrich, *Germany and the Ottoman Empire*, 1914-1918, Princeton, 1968.

VRATSIAN, Simon, *Hayastani Hanrapetutiun* (The Republic of Armenia), 2nd Ed., Beirut, 1958.

WALKER, Christopher, J., *Armenia: the Survival of a Nation*, London, 1990.

WERFEL, Franz, *The Forty Days of Musa Dagh*, trans. G. Dunlop, London, 1934.

ZENKOVSKY, Serge A., *Pan-Turkism and Islam in Russia*, Cambridge, Mass., 1960.

# INDEX

Abbas the Great, Shah, 17, 79
Abgar, King of Edessa, 15
Adana, 7, 25, 38
Africa, 57
AGBU: see Armenian General
 Benevolent Union
Aghanbegian, Abel, 121
Aghdam, 91, 92, 115, 118
Aghvank: see Albania
Aimee, Anouk, 51
Aivazian, Suren, 120-21
Aktarian, Virgile, 54
Albania, kingdom of, 74, 75,
 76-77, 80
Albanian language, 75-76
Aleppo, 12, 56
Alexander II, Tsar, 31
Alexander III, Tsar, 85
Alexander the Good, Prince, 16
Alexandretta, 37
Alexandropol, 35, 85, 89, 97,
 105
Ali, Muhammad, 56
Aliev, Haidar, 121, 122
Alik, 55
All-Armenian National Move-
 ment, 66
Allied High Commission, 97
Allied Powers, 33, 93, 97-98
Anatolia, 9, 16, 17, 27, 41, 103,
 111
Andranik, 88, 90, 91, 93, 94,
 95, 106, 126

Ankara, 3, 28, 106, 111
Antioch, 28
Amaras Monastery, 75
Arabs, 71, 76, 77
Ararat, 9, 17, 117
Araxes river, 8, 71, 1114
Ardahan, 7, 22, 32, 34, 61
ARF: see Dashnak party
Argentina, 51
Argyll, Duke of, 22
Armenakans of Van, 23
Armenia, 3, 7-9, 69-71, 75;
 kingdom of, 15-16, 51, 73-
 74, 76-77; medieval, 16-17,
 34, 37, 40-41, 70, 78-79:
 Republic of, 5, 32-34, 50, 61,
 64, 89, 91, 94, 97, 99-100,
 123, 126; Russian, 83-86, 87;
 sovietization of, 34, 99, 105-
 6, 118; Turkic population of,
 97, 128, 134: see also Arme-
 nian Soviet Socialist Repub-
 lic, Eastern Armenia, Great
 Armenia, Lesser Armenia,
 Turkish Armenia, Western
 Armenia
Armenian alphabet, 15, 75
Armenian Apostolic Church,
 10, 12, 15-16; in diaspora,
 51, 52-54, 55, 56-57; in
 Ottoman Empire, 17, 20, 26;
 in Russia, 31, 85-86; split,
 13; in Turkey, 38-41, 46, 47

147

report series. It is only with the help of our supporters that we are able to pursue our aims and objectives – to secure justice for disadvantaged groups around the world.

We currently offer a reduced annual rate for individual subscribers – please ring our Subscription Desk on 071 978 9498 for details. Payment can be easily made by MasterCard or Visa over the telephone or by post.

All enquiries to:   Sales Department
The Minority Rights Group
379 Brixton Road
London
SW9 7DE
United Kingdom.

Customers in North America wishing to purchase copies of our reports should contact:
Cultural Survival
53 Church Street
Cambridge
MA 02138
USA